I'll Do It Tomorrow

D1507044

I'll Do It Tomorrow

How To Stop Putting It Off and Get It Done Today

© Creator's Syndicate, Inc.

Jerry & Kirsti Newcombe

ILLUSTRATIONS BY **Johnny Hart**

BROADMAN
&HOLMAN
PUBLISHERS

Nashville, Tennessee

© 1999 by Jerry and Kirsti Newcombe

All rights reserved
Printed in the United States of America

0-8054-1267-0 (pbk.)

Published by Broadman & Holman Publishers, Nashville, Tennessee
Editorial Team: Vicki Crumpton, Janis Whipple, Kim Overcash
Design and Typesetting: TF Designs, Mt. Juliet, Tennessee

Dewey Decimal Classification: 640
Subject Heading: TIME MANAGEMENT/PROCRASTINATION
Library of Congress Card Catalog Number: 98-50394

All BC comics are used by permission from Creators Syndicate, Inc.

Unless otherwise stated all Scripture citation is from the NIV, the Holy Bible, New International
Version, copyright © 1973, 1978, 1984 by International Bible Society.

Library of Congress Cataloging-in-Publication Data
Newcombe, Jerry.
        I'll do it tomorrow : how to stop putting it off and get it done today /
Jerry and Kirsti Newcombe
                p. cm.
        Includes bibliographical references and an index.
        ISBN 0-8054-1267-0 (pbk.)
        1. Time Management—Religious aspects—Christianity. 2. Procrastination—Religious aspects—
Christianity. I. Newcombe, Kirsti,. II. Title
BV4598.5.N48   1999
640'.43—dc21   98-50394
                                                                                      CIP

1 2 3 4 03 02 01 00 99

Dedicated to
Bobby Hart

Acknowledgments

There are many people to thank for this new book. First of all, there's the Hart clan. Johnny, Bobby, and Perri Hart were very helpful and generous throughout the whole process. Johnny's cartoons have kept us in stiches. What a punster!

We're thankful to Mary Ann Veldman, who helped convert this from an idea to reality. Also, we're grateful to Jerry's brother, Rick Newcombe, founder and president of Creators Syndicate, Inc.

Finally, thanks go out to the delightful team at Broadman & Holman, including Bucky Rosenbaum, Mark Lusk, Vicki Crumpton, Janis Whipple, et al.

Since this problem (procrastination) is really Jerry's issue (as opposed to Kirsti's), the "I" and "me" throughout the book is Jerry. Kirsti seems to have been born organized!

CONTENTS

© Creators Syndicate, Inc.

Part I: A Brief
Look at Procrastination

© Creators Syndicate, Inc.

Part II: Six Keys to Overcoming Procrastination

© Creators Syndicate, Inc.

Part One

A BRIEF LOOK AT PROCRASTINATION

© Creators Syndicate, Inc.

Chapter 1

© Creators Syndicate, Inc.

A SILENT THIEF ON THE LOOSE

Procrastination is the thief of time. Collar him!
—Charles Dickens

There's a silent thief stalking the land. He steals more money—in lost productivity alone—than the Mafia could ever get their hands on. He steals more joy and happiness than what we collectively experience at Christmas. He steals the peace of mind of many a soul and leaves a wake of guilt. He even steals life itself from those who put off seeking proper medical help. Chances are this silent thief is stealing from you! The name of this thief is, of course, procrastination.

© Creators Syndicate, Inc. But wait a minute. Isn't procrastination just a funny, harmless foible? Well, yes and no. Procrastination is the one vice that we often laugh off, but in the end the laugh is on us.

Do you, like me (especially when I was younger), tend to procrastinate? Are you a "putter-offer"? Who doesn't procrastinate to some degree? On the other hand, there are many who procrastinate quite severely, and they pay a high price for their vice. This book is for procrastinators of all levels—from the occasional procrastinator to the person with a serious problem in this area. Obviously a lot of people have problems with procrastination—ask any accountant on April 15!

Did you know that there are some fourteen thousand dues-paying members of the Procrastinators Club of America, which has its headquarters outside of Philadelphia? And I'm sure there are a lot more who've been thinking of joining, but they just haven't gotten around to it.

HOW TO KNOW IF YOU'RE A PROCRASTINATOR

So how do you know if this is your issue? Well, you know you're a procrastinator if:

- 🕐 you bought this book six months ago and you're just *now* getting around to reading it.
- 🕐 you do your taxes by April 15, that were due the *previous* April 15.

- you buy everything but the turkey for your Thanksgiving meal at 7-11—on Thanksgiving Day.
- you do all your Christmas shopping on December 24—and 25.
- you hand deliver your Christmas cards, sometime around New Year's Day.
- you can't pay a bill without simultaneously paying late charges.
- you always have to bring money with you when you finally return a library book, in order to cover the late fee.
- you went through high school and college always asking for an extension on your assignments.
- you're an expert at coming up with all sorts of excuses for being late.
- you find yourself sharpening all your pencils, and everyone else's while you're at it, rather than writing that overdue report.
- your work area is cluttered with reams of paperwork. Mixed together in the stack are both urgent and unimportant items; and some of the papers are stuck together with the remains of last Tuesday's breakfast.
- you visit the dentist only when you feel the pain of a cavity.
- you hit your snooze button five times before you get out of bed.
- at bedside, you have a mound of books each of which you started to read but never finished.
- you find 1,001 things to do before you tackle the task at hand.

If this describes you in any way, take heart, fellow procrastinator. There's hope for change. And the rewards for change are exhilarating! The entire quality of one's life improves when procrastination is in check. I should know, for I have struggled with this problem for years, and I've learned some principles and insights that have helped me overcome it . . . by-and-large.

"OF TOMORROW"

Procrastination comes from the Latin words meaning "of tomorrow." But personally, I like Don Marquis's definition better. He said procrastination is the "art of keeping up with yesterday." That has been about my speed.

MY (MOSTLY FORMER) PROCRASTINATION HABIT

For many years I have struggled with the problem of procrastinating. I went through the early part of college putting off my studying until the last minute. Then I'd have to pull an all-nighter to catch up.

My procrastination habit led to my only known instance of sleepwalking. I

had stayed up all night to study for a test. After I took the exam in the morning, I took an afternoon nap. While I was still asleep, I got up and for some strange reason put on my roommate's pants. (I think I put on his pants because they were the only ones that were laying out at the time.) And then, without shirt or shoes, I walked through the campus quad at Tulane University all the way to the library, which was at least

© Creators Syndicate, Inc.

two long blocks away. I walked up to the third floor and sat in my usual cubicle. As I shivered because of the air-conditioning, I tried to read some book that happened to be laying on the desk. I couldn't understand a thing as I tried reading and rereading the same sentence. It was a tome about advanced calculus or the like. As I kept trying to make sense of the blurred words, I suddenly woke up! I realized where I was, what I had done, and what had happened. Being the prude that I am, I was embarrassed being shirtless in the library. To this day, I don't know how I was able to get in without being turned away at the door. I quickly, furtively walked back—hoping not to get noticed by anyone I knew, as I strode through the crowded quad.

There were to be a few more all-nighters after that, but after a while, I started budgeting my time better so as to avoid them.

THE BLOWN OPPORTUNITIES

The sadder aspect of procrastination is the blown opportunities. I've cheated myself out of great things by postponing the important things. When I was a senior in high school, the drama department was putting on the elaborate musical *Fiddler on the Roof*. There were two parts I wanted—Tevye, the lead, or Model, an important supporting role. Physically and voice-wise, I had a good shot at Model (pronounced MOW-duhl). I fantasized about having either of these good roles. I dreamed about all the attention that would be lavished on me. And I even wrote the goal down on paper. But did I practice? Not really. I found time for just about everything else, while in the back of my mind I remembered I should practice. Needless to say, I didn't get either part. Even if I had practiced a lot, I might not have gotten a leading role, but chances would have been much better. Instead, I ended up getting a very small part. You've probably never heard of it, even if you're familiar with *Fiddler on the Roof*. I played the hatmaker; I had three lines. I still had to make the serious time commitment to the play; I still had to attend all the rehearsals just as much as the

HALT! WHO GOES THERE?

SIR JOHN, "THE SLOW," BEARING A PLUMP GRAPE FOR QUEEN IDA'S BIRTHDAY

...LOOKS LIKE A DRIED-UP RAISIN TO ME!

"WHEN IT ABSOLUTELY HAS TO BE THERE OVERNIGHT" IS NOT ONE OF MY MAIN SLOGANS.

© Creators Syndicate, Inc.

other characters. But by postponing serious practice before the auditions, I had cheated myself out of the possibility of a good role.

Because of procrastination, many people miss out on serious opportunities, such as:

- 🕐 The person who has an important job interview and who fails to prepare sufficiently.
- 🕐 The homemaker who claims she wants to spend more time with her child but takes the easy route and watches the soaps on TV.
- 🕐 The businessman who has put off for years making that helpful suggestion that could improve the company's profits. He's waiting for *just* the right timing—only to see someone else propose a similar idea and then see them advance right up.

Think of the many good deeds left undone because of procrastination. Think of the unreconciled relationships needing forgiveness and healing. The road to hell, it is said, is paved with good intentions. Indeed, a silent thief stalks the land!

Procrastination is a thief. It robs us of many of the great things life has to offer. It robs us of peace of mind, giving us instead guilt feelings about important things left undone. It defrauds us of joy, of security, and in some cases, even of life itself—as in the case of those who put off cancer-detection examinations. For most people, procrastination will

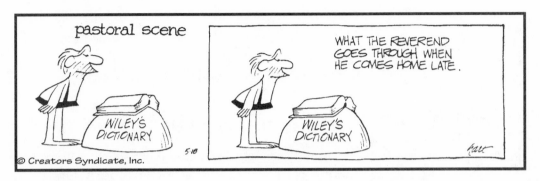

pastoral scene

WILEY'S DICTIONARY

© Creators Syndicate, Inc.

5·18

WHAT THE REVEREND GOES THROUGH WHEN HE COMES HOME LATE.

WILEY'S DICTIONARY

not wreak such severe havoc, but it does rob us of living up to our potential. Lee Buck, in his book *Tapping Your Secret Source of Power,* tells about a procrastinator, whom he calls "Zach." Zach set out to write an important biography of George Washington Carver. Carver, you will recall, was the African-American scientist who did ground-breaking studies on the peanut, which "helped rejuvenate the economy of southern agriculture, once totally dependent on cotton."[1] As Zach did his research, he found his subject fascinating. Every time Lee saw him, he'd ask how the book was going. Zach would enthusiastically respond, "Great, I'm starting on it right away." Or he'd say, "Don't expect to see much of me after next week because that's when I'm really going to get cracking on it."

But the book never materialized, and a few years later, Lee sat down to read the paper and came across a review of a book by *another* author on George Washington Carver. By putting off and putting off, Zach had missed out on a great opportunity. He had missed out on enriching all of us by the work he might have accomplished.

From this experience, Lee Buck surmises:

> All too often I have heard good ideas expounded at luncheon tables and then, when not acted upon, turn up in another company where they have been put to good use. . . . How many scientists before Jonas Salk

came along, I wonder, were on the verge of discovering a polio vaccine, only to fall prey to some form of delay? How many lives would have been saved if they had diligently followed up their leads?[2]

OVERCOMING PROCRASTINATION

If you struggle with procrastination, I believe you'll find this book helpful. This in turn could lead to a more fulfilling life—a life with greater potential and excitement. If you follow the simple steps outlined in this book, you may well find yourself achieving all sorts of accomplishments that just a few years ago you would have thought impossible!

When it comes to writing a book on procrastination, I consider myself an expert—not necessarily on how to overcome it, but on how to do it! I still have the *tendency*—left to my natural state—to put things off. But, by the grace of God, I have improved a lot in this area. In this book, I will share insights and principles that help us lick the procrastination habit before it licks us!

Thus, the purpose of this book is to provide habit-changing principles in a non-threatening way to both serious and occasional procrastinators. The goal is to present the information in a light and easy-to-digest manner. If you don't put off reading the rest of this book, I will have succeeded greatly in the first part of my goal for this little volume. If you apply one or two of the principles, I will have made it to second base. But if you apply many or all of these ideas, and subsequently get your habit of procrastination in check, I will have hit a home run!

THE BENEFITS OF NOT PROCRASTINATING

There are many reasons to stop procrastinating. The benefits should be obvious. Your goals—and maybe you don't even have any because you've been putting off setting any—will not be fulfilled if you have a serious problem with procrastination. The job promotion and pay raise you desire will go to the younger, more aggressive man or woman in the office—the one who knows how to manage him or herself better than you do.

This touches on an important area—self-management. Learning to overcome procrastination involves managing yourself—controlling yourself; acting, not responding; deciding, not being decided upon; being proactive, not reactive. Brian Tracy, the motivational speaker and author of *Maximum Achievement,* points out: "We will set our own

© Creators Syndicate, Inc.

goals or we'll have them set for us."[3] When you overcome the procrastination habit, you will start achieving more and more of your potential.

Imagine the feeling of being on top of your schedule. Picture yourself free from the guilt of having left many significant things undone. Picture yourself having undertaken and fulfilled an important obligation that has been hanging over you for months, maybe even years! Imagine the satisfaction of completing a long-overdue job.

© Creators Syndicate, Inc.

Another benefit of overcoming procrastination can be financial freedom. It comes from not postponing a budget, which comes from planning ahead on your finances, instead of going from one financial crisis to another. Imagine the feeling you would have if you were financially caught up and you were saving money in the bank. Financial freedom can bring peace of mind.

A QUICK OVERVIEW OF THIS BOOK

Chapters two and three will explore the pros and cons of procrastination. The pros of procrastination? After all of the above, it may seem odd that I would have a chapter about the case for procrastination. However, there is a time to put off, to postpone, to delay a decision. But generally procrastination is harmful. Chapters four and five will look at the causes of and excuses for procrastination.

Part two of this book—"Steps to Overcoming Procrastination"—offers six major strategies that, when applied, will help one curb the "I'll do it tomorrow" syndrome. The first strategy in overcoming procrastination involves deciding what's really important. Some things we put off never have to be done at all; so this chapter will deal with establishing priorities and determining what we really need or want to do in the first place. The second strategy is the time-honored principle of "divide and conquer." We often put off tasks because they seem so formidable; however, when we break them down into smaller parts, we can get anything done. How do you eat an elephant? One bite at a time.

The third strategy I call "the Stonewall Jackson principle." There is a wonderful answer to overcoming procrastination found in the brilliant strategy of one of America's greatest military geniuses. An incredible military leader, Stonewall Jackson was able to defeat an army of some 175,000 with an army of 17,500 that had significantly fewer resources. How? His secret is a key to help procrastinators overcome their problem. It was a big help for me.

The fourth way to overcome the procrastination habit involves creating realistic but challenging deadlines. It's amazing how many things we can achieve if we have deadlines looming over us. I know I have accomplished some things in a short time period I wouldn't have thought possible *only* because I had some deadlines I *had* to meet.

The fifth key to overcoming procrastination involves doing the unpleasant but necessary tasks first. When your mom told you to eat your vegetables before the ice cream, that was not just good nutritional advice; the principle applies to life in general and can help free the procrastinator from this nasty habit. However, this principle must be applied slowly and with caution—lest the hardcore procrastinator get scared off. In addition, it's beneficial to reward yourself at different intervals with predetermined compensations. The sixth strategy involves accountability—both human and divine.

Following these six strategies will liberate average procrastinators from bad habits and get them on the track to success. Each of these chapters will have a few practical exercises—but nothing too difficult or time-consuming. I've put off finishing a few books myself because they've had too many exercises! I don't want to scare anyone away.

A final chapter will put together all the main points of the book. It will also go over a few final considerations. Having made it that far, I trust you too will begin to get the procrastination habit under control.

CONCLUSION

Have you ever heard of a "stove job"? A couple was going to get away for a weekend. They had their special plans all laid out. While he was at work, she was to pack the suitcase. She had every intention of doing so, but she didn't know where to start, and her stove, being as dirty as it was, bothered her. So instead of packing, she spent many hours cleaning and polishing the stove. By the time he came home from work, the stove was sparkling but nothing was ready, and they missed their trip. Doing a "stove job" means being busily engaged in one activity—perhaps a worthwhile one—when you should have been doing the task at hand. Unfortunately, many people go through life doing one stove job after another. I hope and pray that through this book you may learn a few principles that will enable you to avoid doing stove jobs—except when cleaning the stove is the task at hand!

I hope that you will take some of these principles and make them your own, and thus keep the silent thief of procrastination at bay. Let the comedians make their jokes about procrastination. I hope you will be able to laugh along with them and not allow yourself to be the punchline.

Chapter 2

© Creators Syndicate, Inc.

PROCRASTINATION CAN BE HAZARDOUS TO YOUR HEALTH

Only two things come to him who waits: whiskers and bills.
—Anonymous

O n a winter day many years ago, an eagle spotted the dead carcass of an animal floating on a bed of ice along the Niagara River toward the falls. He swooped down and landed on the cake of ice and started eating. Even though he was floating toward the precipice, apparently he perceived no imminent danger, for he could fly away at a moment's notice. So the eagle delayed his departure as he continued to eat his prey. But when he got so close to the falls that it was time to fly away, he found that he couldn't! Unknown to him, his talons had frozen in the ice, and he couldn't free them, try as he might. He flapped furiously but to no avail. And he plunged to his death . . . a death caused by procrastination!

Now this example may seem extreme. But suffice it to say there are some bad consequences to procrastination.

Virtually all historians of the U.S. Civil War regard Gettysburg as the turning point of that conflict. But did you know that many of them (albeit, indirectly) cite procrastination as one of the key reasons the South lost that crucial battle? Many historians believe that Confederate General James Longstreet was partially responsible for the Gettysburg defeat because he delayed his attack on the second day of the three-day battle—although Robert E. Lee gave him clear orders to attack in the morning. Longstreet, it is reported, was upset that General Lee had not chosen his alternative battle plan, so he dragged his feet. With his delay, the Union forces were able to fortify their strongholds, making them impenetrable to Southern attack. By the time Longstreet attempted his attack—at four o'clock in the afternoon—it was way too late. They were easily repulsed. Then, on the third day of the battle, George Picket's charge was to be early in the morning. That too was delayed—with disastrous consequences. General Lee's plan for an audacious attack turned into a suicide mission, in large part because of procrastination. Not all historians would necessarily agree with this simplistic interpretation, but I find it interesting because it's another example of how procrastination leads to failure and misery.

© Creators Syndicate, Inc.

THE MISSED OPPORTUNITIES

Sadly, many people go through life with a trail of missed opportunities. They leave a wake of "might have beens." They never live up to their God-given potential. As Oliver Wendell Holmes once said, the average person goes to his grave with his music still in him.[1] Zig Ziglar adds, "unfortunately, the most beautiful melodies of all are the unplayed ones."[2]

A frustrating aspect of procrastination is that by continually putting things off, you can essentially allow life to pass you by! There is an old legend of a princess who loses because she puts off making a decision. According to the fairy tale, the princess is allowed to walk through a field covered with beautiful jewels; and she has the privilege of picking one, but only one, that she can keep. She is allowed to walk through the field only once, and she can only go forward, not backwards (just like life). As she begins her journey, she sees diamonds, rubies, emeralds, and sapphires glittering in the sun. She sees pearls as big as cherries. Everywhere she looks, she sees gems shining brilliantly. But she thinks that she mustn't choose so early because surely they will get brighter and bigger. But as she continues her walk, the brilliance of the jewels slowly begins to fade. They also seem to be getting smaller. So she postpones her choice, holding out for something bigger. After a while, she nears the end of the field. But now, they seem like dime-store glass and not worth having. So she doesn't choose any of these. Before she knows it, the princess is out of the Field of Gems, and she hasn't picked one. And then it's too late. Life can be like that for the procrastinator. Tomorrow, tomorrow. But tomorrow may never come. A bird in the hand really is worth two in the bush.

I think the person the procrastinator cheats most is him or herself. We have to settle for second best because we put off the key steps to success. James Albery puts it this way:

> He slept beneath the moon,
> He basked beneath the sun,

He lived a life of going-to-do
And died with nothing done.[3]

THE PROCRASTINATOR PAYS MORE—
IN LATE FEES AND OTHER EXPENSES

But procrastination does not just lead to Opportunity Lost. It also leads to late fees and penalties. Suppose you do your grocery shopping at a local convenience store because you put it off and now it's too late. The other stores are closed. You have to pay through the nose—$3.00 for a bag of chips? Shucks, you could have gotten that at the grocery store for $1.59. At these prices, maybe it's best to *not* put off that diet. And that gallon of milk. Does it really have to cost $4.00? That's a dollar short of a fiver!

Look at the late penalties for paying your mortgage. Mine is about $35.00. You can buy a lot of bubble gum with $35.00!

Sometimes you can pay double for procrastinating your payments. In April 1993, I got a speeding ticket in Colorado Springs. I couldn't believe how small it was! It was only $13.00. When the officer gave it to me, I said, "Wow, I want to move here." But a colleague who was there tells me that I said, "Wow, can I have another one?" Anyway, as cheap as it was (I felt like we were in a time warp), there was a time limit as to when it was to be paid. And did I pay it on time? Noooooooooooo. I ended up putting it off. They returned my check and sent me a new bill. Only this time it was $29.00. Imagine that. Just by putting off payment for a few weeks, I had to pay more than double the amount! Take that example and multiply it out all over the place and you see what I mean by late fees.

Look at all the last-minute shopping that goes on at Christmas and the higher prices one has to pay at such a time. With characteristic tongue-in-cheek, syndicated columnist Molly Ivins prefaced one of her last-minute shoppers' guides this way:

LOOK AT ALL THOSE POOR FOOLS SCURRYING AROUND DOING THEIR LAST-MINUTE SHOPPING. ...BOY, WE REALLY PLAYED IT SMART THIS YEAR, KID.

HOW'S THAT?

BY AGREEING NOT TO BUY GIFTS FOR EACH OTHER.

THAT'S RIGHT.

12-24

WHAAAAAAAHHHH

© Creators Syndicate, Inc.

"Fellow slackers, here again, in the nick of St. Nick, it's the annual Procrastinators' Christmas Book List! Please note how early the list is this year: one week ahead of time, a new record. I hope it's not too early—you know we have always lost *The New York Times Christmas Book List* by the time we get around to shopping. Why they persist in putting it out a month early is beyond me. But as you also know, the thought of Christmas shopping does not equal the deed, and I, too, will be out on Christmas Eve, in the drugstore, trying to figure out whether my nearest and dearest would prefer Fixodent to deodorant in celebration of the seasonal joy."[4]

More often than not, there's a price to pay for procrastination.

THE U.S. ECONOMY, PUTTING OFF THE HARD CHOICES

The U.S. government for years has been putting off the hard choices of what to cut from our budget. So we've been spending and spending like there's no tomorrow. What this has come to mean is that each baby born today owes to the federal government about $70,000. Just for being born? How could this be? We've been putting off the hard choices and taking the path of least resistance. A political cartoon in *World* magazine illustrated the cause of this problem well. It showed a man with a placard that contained Patrick Henry's well-known slogan on it: "Give me liberty or give me death." Only, the words *liberty*, *or,* and *death* were crossed off; so the sign actually read: "Give me, give me." In two hundred short years, we've gone from "Give me liberty or give me death" to just plain "Give me, give me!"

The U.S. government owes a ton of bucks. Nearly 22 percent of the budget in 1996 went to pay off interest on the money we've borrowed.[5] We're living way beyond our means. The national debt is now in excess of six trillion dollars. That's hard to realize. But think of a trillion dollars this way. If you could go back to the time of Christ and spend one million dollars a day, seven days a week, from that time until the present—one million dollars every single day!—by the year 2000 you still wouldn't have reached one trillion dollars!!! And we owe six times that! Yipes!

© Creators Syndicate, Inc.

PROCRASTINATION WITH WIDESPREAD RESULTS

Another example of the downside of procrastination run amok is the whole Y2K (year two thousand) computer mess. At *least* since the early 1980s, technicians and programmers could have fixed computers so that the rollover from 1999 to 2000 would have been a non-event. But nooooooooo. Y2K became the most expensive problem in human history. Worldwide estimates to make our computers ready for the next millennium range from $600 billion to $1 trillion dollars—with Y2K-related litigation expected to far exceed that amount. Whatever chaos, inconvenience, and economic downturn Y2K has caused and will continue to cause, you can essentially attribute to the "I'll do it tomorrow" syndrome.

PROCRASTINATION IN THE REALM OF PERSONAL FINANCES

We seem to be a society run on credit. But to borrow an expression from Shakespeare, "neither a lender, nor a borrower be."

Financial adviser Larry Burkett shows how the misuse of credit is a form of procrastination:

> In our society today you can borrow to buy things that you can't afford to own. And credit doesn't eliminate the decision that you can't afford to own—it only delays it and makes it worse. . . . Unfortunately, it's a lot of fun to get into debt because you can buy things that you don't have to have and you can buy things that you can't afford to own.[6]

© Creators Syndicate, Inc.

The credit card becomes a key instrument to procrastination: It postpones the true decision of whether you can afford something or not. Can you? If you can't, then using the credit card will just jack up the price. Here's a famous conversation you'll *never* hear: "Oh, look, Henry, they have these dresses on sale now, 10 percent off. . . . Let's use our credit card and buy them and we'll pay 18 percent interest—thus, 30 percent more by the time we pay it off!" A lot of shoppers don't seem to realize that the savings gained by the sale prices are nullified by the interest they pay on the credit card.

The Federal Reserve System reports that outstanding consumer credit rose from $133 billion in 1970 to $809 billion in 1992 to $1.2 trillion in 1996. This means as a nation we're living by borrowing. I'm not saying anything's wrong with borrowing per se or using credit cards (when paid off monthly). What I am saying is (and really I'm just echoing Burkett and others on this point) the misuse of credit can be. It is bad when you postpone the decision of whether you can afford to own something and you go ahead and buy it anyway! One day it'll all catch up with you.

Another area where procrastination causes damage in finances is in the lack of long-term savings. Have you ever seen those incredible charts where if you save $X for retirement when you're twenty, you will have earned gazillions because of the compound interest? But if you save the same thing starting at the age of thirty—or worse, forty—you only earn a fraction of the amount. Nonetheless, apart from unusual disruptions to the economy, it's still better to start saving no matter what the age. Unfortunately, many Americans don't save enough for their retirement. This is, of course, a symptom of procrastination. Marketing Research Institute did a study on this and found that as a whole, we are saving about one-third less than what we'll need to retire in the way we would like. They reported that Baby Boomers in particular were doing a poor job of saving for the future. One official from the organization that cosponsored the survey said that there were many indications people were increasingly aware of "the crisis in retirement savings." However, they themselves were still not *doing* anything to adequately prepare for retirement![7]

TAKING CARE OF YOURSELF

We often ignore or put things off that would make us healthier. I drifted through much of my childhood without undergoing the nightly ritual of brushing my teeth. It caught up with me every time I went to the dentist. I'd have one, two, or even three cavities. But one day, when I was in third grade, I went to the dentist, and after learning I had to get two or three fillings, it finally dawned on me that it was really up to *me* whether or not I would get cavities. So from that day on, I have brushed my teeth daily. Never again, I resolved, would I go through the agony of that drilling!

Perhaps more effective than brushing is flossing your teeth. I'll never forget what one dentist said to me: "You don't have to floss your teeth every day—only the ones you want to keep!" I confess I have too often put off his excellent advice. But I'll get around to it one of these days.

© Creators Syndicate, Inc.

Millions of Americans put off losing weight. They know they should for their health's sake. They know they should for the sake of their appearance. They know they should for their wardrobe's sake. But they postpone the inevitable. I should know—I've been struggling with this one for a while.[8] Americans spend BIG BUCKS on diets. This is a strong testimony to the fact that millions are putting off losing that weight.

Another thing many procrastinators put off, with potentially fatal consequences, is quitting smoking. They want to. And they will. One of these days. One of these years. It's tough, I'm sure. I'm not addicted to nicotine, but I am somewhat addicted to coffee.[9]

Meanwhile, researchers reveal that *the majority* of the 44 million Americans or so who smoke wish they did not. (One challenge I give to my kids so they'll hopefully never light up is: Find me one adult who smokes cigarettes who didn't wish they could stop.) According to Tom Heymann in *The Unofficial U.S. Census,* 17,300,000 smokers will quit this year—at least for one day. But only 1,300,000 of these will truly quit—at least for a year.[10] Fortunately, there are many people, millions in fact, who have successfully stopped smoking, even when it was a habit for years. Putting off quitting can be fatal. Meanwhile, there are positive benefits to kicking this habit. It's amazing how forgiving our body can be even if we have abused it by smoking.[11]

POTENTIALLY FATAL CONSEQUENCES TO PROCRASTINATION

One last major consequence of procrastination can be premature death. I knew a woman who is no longer

© Creators Syndicate, Inc.

with us. She died a horrible, painful death. It didn't take one or two years. It took nearly a decade. It was breast cancer. She was so busy making a living, she neglected to be test-ed regularly until it was too late. She and her husband had big plans for what they would do in their retirement years which were right around the corner. In fact, they were all set to buy an R.V. and tour the country. Instead, their time and savings were consumed by her frequent trips to the hospital and operations, on the oxygen tanks and medicines. The only touring they did was of the medical ward. It was tragic. This is not in any way to say that all cancers can be prevented, but many can be with early detection.

Here's the amazing thing: There are about as many survivors of cancer today, living in America, as it would take to populate a large, metropolitan city. For example, there are currently as many survivors of cancer as could populate the city of Los Angeles within the city limits! The key is early detection. All joking aside, procrastination can be fatal to your health. Get check-ups regularly.

© Creators Syndicate, Inc.

SPIRITUAL PROCRASTINATION

Another type of bankruptcy that can result from procrastination out of control is spir-itual bankruptcy. I remember reading a story in the paper about a pilot whose airplane went down. The pilot said in an interview that it all happened so fast there wasn't even time to *pray*. Wow! He said everything happened within eleven seconds and that he was "totally occupied" during that time. He also said he believed God intervened anyway and spared them from certain death.[12] No time to pray? That leads me to my point: Putting off important spiritual commitments can be hazardous to your soul.

I remember talking with a friend in college about spiritual things. He told me he knew all about his need to make peace with God, but that he was going to wait until he was on his deathbed before doing that. But I told him, to no avail (at least as far as I know), that that was spiritually dangerous. What if he were to die in a car accident in a split second? You can't count on tomorrow. (If you need to make peace with God, please see the Appendix on "Something Really Important to Not Put Off.")

Nolbert Hunt Quayle once wrote this of procrastination: "'Tomorrow!' is the devil's motto. Earth's history is strewn with the wrecks of half-finished plans and unexecuted resolution. 'Tomorrow' is the perpetual refuge of incompetency and sloth."[13]

CONCLUSION

So there are indeed many harmful consequences to procrastination. Perhaps the saddest are the people who leave a wake of "might have beens." I might have been this. I might have done that. But, thankfully, there is a chance to change before it's too late . . . as it was for Colonel Rahl.

One day during the American War for Independence, when the Hessian army was encamped in Trenton, their commander, Colonel Rahl, was busily engaged in playing cards and focusing on their fun when suddenly someone came up and handed him a letter. Unbeknownst to him, the message of that letter could have saved his life! But he simply put it in his pocket to read later and continued on with the game. The message he put off reading was a communique (sent by a British sympathizer) that stated that George Washington was crossing the Delaware River. Instead of reading it right away, the colonel waited until the game was over. But by then it was too late to rally his troops. He was killed, and his men were taken prisoner. The game of life was over, and he had lost. Procrastination can have dire consequences!

Chapter 3

© Creators Syndicate, Inc.

THE PROS OF PROCRASTINATION

Always put off until tomorrow what you are going to make a mess of today.
—Anonymous

A couple of years ago I called the Procrastinators Club of America and spoke with a gentleman who was supposed to be elected as their president. They haven't gotten around to voting on it yet. I asked for an application, and he promised to send me one. I'm sure I'll get it one of these days, or months, or whatever. He seemed shocked when I asked to get it it by Christmas (we spoke in the summer). He prided himself in telling me that procrastinators live longer and enjoy life more than nonprocrastinators. "What research would back that up?" I asked. He said that procrastinators tend to be Type B personalities. They don't work themselves up in a frenzy, rushing off in haste from this thing to that, accomplishing many things that perhaps are best left undone. Procrastinators, said he, stop and take time to smell the roses.

Is he right? Do procrastinators have more fun? I don't know. Ask the people waiting in line at the post office on April 15!

Despite all we've said in the first and second chapters and all that we will go on to say in the rest of the book, there *is* a time to procrastinate, to put off, to postpone. Remember bygone times when people would sit around on their front porch and chit-chat about the latest? Perhaps such relaxing times are viewed by Type As as a total waste of time. I'm not so sure. I think there is a time to stop, to slow down, to "shoot the breeze." Now if that's all you did, that wouldn't be good!

In this chapter, we want to explore several scenarios where it makes sense to procrastinate. Included in this category is waiting until you have the best deal. Also, if you are job hunting, it makes a lot of sense to look rather carefully before you change positions. It would be a fiasco to turn in a good job for a poor one that perhaps looked good at first glance.

© Creators Syndicate, Inc.

© Creators Syndicate, Inc.

NOT SELLING YOURSELF SHORT

One time when we may want to strategically delay is when we are negotiating. What do experts say is the key to effective negotiations? Being willing to walk away from the deal, after clearly stating your case. If the other side won't budge and you've reached the point where you think it unwise to budge any further, then it's time to walk away. This walking away is, in a sense, a form of procrastination; putting off completing the deal. But isn't it better to put off a poor deal than to consummate one you don't want in the first place?

Consider this example from the early days of the movies. One of the greatest comics who ever lived was Buster Keaton. His silent comedies—from *Cops* to *The General*—are outstanding and innovative. He used his total body in excellent pantomime and gestures. He did his own stunt work, which was phenomenal and at times life-threatening. Unfortunately, he was one of those who did not make a successful transition from silent movies to talkies. Buster Keaton's problem was that he chose to go with a compromised deal, and it killed his career.

Although he had had a prosperous and profitable decade in the 1920s, Buster Keaton's business manager and financier called it quits and struck out on his own. This effectively dissolved the arrangement by which Keaton had been free to create his innovative work. Meanwhile, Keaton received a job offer from MGM. It may have looked good at the time, but some warned against it. His personal friend and rival at the box office, Charlie Chaplin, forewarned him that if he took that position, he'd lose out because he'd lose his creative control over his films. Instead, the big studio would squeeze him into a formulaic mold they thought the box office wanted. Keaton took the job anyway, and it ruined his career. Instead of holding out for a better offer, which would have likely come given his incredible recent success, he chose the path of least resistance. It has been said, "The path of least resistance leads to the path of least reward." This move was not only disastrous to Keaton's career: It ruined his marriage and everything else because he turned to the bottle for solace. There is a time to wait and a time to delay.

I think another area that calls for procrastinating is in consumer purchases (as opposed to things needed for your business). Some things are cheaper after they've been on the market for a little while. For example, take electronic gizmos. Often the price of computers and computer-related products goes down significantly over time. Even waiting a year or so can lead to substantial savings. I remember when a friend of mine in high school bought an electronic calculator for $174. Recently, my wife bought a similar type of calculator (even the same brand) for $9! I like going to dollar theaters, as opposed·to first-run cinemas. What's the big deal if you wait a few weeks? It's rare for me to go to a first-run movie. Put it off, and often you pay far less.

LIVING IN DAYTIGHT COMPARTMENTS

There are some time management experts who appear to be so uptight and high-powered that they seem to have every little move they're going to make planned ahead. I

© Creators Syndicate, Inc.

don't see how you can live like that. It certainly doesn't build in any room for the unexpected. And let's face it, the unexpected is often a part of our daily lives. Someone once said, "Life is what happens to you when you're planning something else!" I think that's often true. So, if you're not sure whether you should do XYZ, then consider it, pray about it, analyze it, talk to the right people about it, and go ahead and give it time . . . which is another way of saying, put off your decision if you need to. That may well be the best decision, given the facts at this very moment. How can you tell if this decision is one you should put off or not? Easy. Do you have all the critical facts you need in the case? If you are lacking key information, then don't make a half-informed decision! By all means put it off.

In His Sermon on the Mount, Jesus said, "Don't worry about tomorrow, for tomorrow will worry about itself. Each day has enough trouble of its own."[1] We often forget that principle, and we take upon ourselves all sorts of anxieties. To worry about the future is not procrastination per se but rather it is borrowing tomorrow's trouble for today. The key is, we need to focus our energies today for

© Creators Syndicate, Inc.

today's tasks. I might add that *planning* for the future and *worrying* about the future are two different matters.

This idea of living each day at a time and not worrying about tomorrow is great advice. As Sir William Osler put it, we should live in "daytight compartments." Dr. D. James Kennedy, pastor of Coral Ridge Presbyterian Church and speaker on *The Coral Ridge Hour*, says:

"We need to focus on the present moment to the exclusion of the past or future. We are to seize the day, the moment, and rejoice and be glad in it. Our happiness is not to be left in the past. Nor are we to wait until tomorrow to be glad. Today, at this very moment we are to exude gladness. Right now pay attention to what is going on. Keep your eye on the ball of life. It is like the art of reading aloud. You must put the impact you want to convey right on the word you are speaking. You cannot let your thoughts race three or four words ahead of what you are actually saying. Doing so causes the words to lose their meaning and impact. Similarly, do not think about rejoicing tomorrow."[2] Think about rejoicing today . . . and do it!

Thus, we should savor each day. The Bible puts it altogether in one simple statement: "This is the day the Lord has made. We will rejoice and be glad in it."[3]

PUT OFF OVERREACTING BEFORE YOU HAVE ALL THE FACTS

Another example where it makes sense to engage in procrastination involves not overreacting to mere appearances. How many times have we blown our stacks at someone, only to discover we didn't have all the facts?

Put off speaking before your mind is engaged! Many times people blurt out their initial reactions to something. It only takes a few seconds, and then they may end up taking hours to try and repair the damage. They may never repair it fully!

There are some situations where it's prudent to avoid hasty decisions. The otherwise wise and godly John Wesley who did so

© Creators Syndicate, Inc.

much good for the cause of Christ in the eighteenth century gives a good example of what *not* to do in the case of marriage. He chose to wed a woman within the first week that he had met her! Although he founded the Methodist Church and helped bring about an important revival in England, his home life was anything but conducive to his ministry. It was a disastrous marriage, and she was a constant obstacle to his work and a constant thorn in his flesh.

We should also avoid jumping on the band wagon on the latest issue without having looked into the matter ourselves. We live in an age of media hype. Take, for example, the sensationalism in the ads for news programs. It would be easy for people to overreact to the hype and blow things out of proportion. Many people have ended up with egg on their faces because they thought the sky was falling when it only turned out to be a minor storm.

PUT OFF CONTINUING,
WHEN YOU'RE JUST SPINNING YOUR WHEELS

Have you ever had the difficult experience of trying to reconcile your bank account, and it won't work no matter what you do? You're just spinning your wheels. Or suppose you're struggling through a complex math problem. No matter how hard you try, you just can't figure it out. You become more frustrated. Finally, you decide to put it off; you lay it aside and take a break. Later you pick it up and try a totally new and fresh approach. Instead of trying through the same well-worn grooves, you start with a new outlook and then it all clicks. This is another example of a good use of procrastination . . . taking a break when it makes sense to do so. Sometimes I've seen business meetings drag on and on very unproductively. It seems that those attending the meeting get stuck with some sort of insurmountable problem, and they can't get beyond it. I would recommend putting off further discussion on that problem.

PUTTING OFF SIN

There is another time for procrastination. This time it should be permanent procrastination. As Mr. Anonymous puts it: "Always put off until tomorrow the things you shouldn't do at all."4 He (or is it she?) also penned these words:

> If you want to keep from trouble,
> Here's a mighty easy way:
> Always put off till tomorrow
> What you shouldn't do today.5

Thus, sin is something that should be put off . . . permanently!

How about sex? That should be put off until marriage. Seriously. For the good of everybody involved. I'm amazed how cavalier people are in their attitudes about this. Just watch TV sometime, and you see people hopping in the sack all the time. In fact, 88 percent of sexual activity in prime-time television is between people who are not married!6 Yet this is something they should postpone for marriage. We did, and we're glad we did.

An interesting finding of that groundbreaking scientific study on sex that was conducted under the auspices of the University of Chicago and released in 1993 was that committed Christians generally report the highest satisfaction with their sex lives. Obviously, being committed Christians, they enjoy sex only in the context of marriage and only with their spouse. Meanwhile, singles out playing the field—the very people supposedly having the "hottest" sex—report "the lowest rates of satisfaction" with their sex lives.[7] Hmmmmm. What can you say? You do things God's way, and everything works out much better.

If you're contemplating an affair with someone else, put it off—forever!

© Creators Syndicate, Inc.

If you're thinking about stealing some of the company funds, put it off—forever!

If you're considering seeking revenge on your neighbor, put it off—forever!

I once heard a story that went something like this. A factory manager went to a motivational seminar on "doing it now." He was all hyped and motivated to "do it now," and he wanted his staff to feel the same way. So he put bumper stickers and posters all over the place that read, "Do It Now!" After a few days, the drill operator punched the foreman;

his best worker quit to work for his competitor; and his chief assistant ran off with the secretary! We don't necessarily want to do it all now. In fact, there are some things we don't want to do. Ever.

There are many times and many areas of our lives where we need to learn self-control. Don't steal. Don't kill. Don't lie. Don't blurt out what you really think of your boss or what you really think of your wife's new hairdo.

And so . . . procrastinate sin—forever!

CONCLUSION

There is a time and a place for everything under the sun. That includes a time for procrastination. I agree with one aspect of the Procrastinators Club of America. If their goal in procrastinating is for people to enjoy life more, then Hear! Hear!

The most common thread of things we should put off are those which need time or those which we should never do! If you have a bunch of things that you've never gotten around to doing, maybe it's because it really doesn't matter that you never get around to doing them! If there are things like that, then perhaps you just need to decide

© Creators Syndicate, Inc.

that it really doesn't matter. So if you get around to it, great. But if not, that's fine too. This way, they won't be a burden to you at all.

If you're not sure whether they should be done or not, then put it off until you can decide later. When in doubt, do without.

Chapter 4

© Creators Syndicate, Inc.

A LION IN THE STREET: CAUSES OF PROCRASTINATION

Every time a man puts a new idea across,
he finds ten men who thought of it before he did
—but only thought of it.
—Advertizer's Digest

n *Do the Right Thing*, a movie by filmmaker Spike Lee, there are a couple of scenes with an indirect message for procrastinators. Early in the movie, we see a family of immigrants, newly arrived in this country, starting a shop, while in the background are some natural-born Americans sitting around talking. Later in the movie, the hard work of the immigrants has paid off. Their store is making money. Meanwhile, the same group of people who were sitting around before are still sitting around, only now they're complaining how unfair it is that they are poor and the store owners are well off. What a great indictment against procrastination!

"I can't go to work," says the sluggard, "there's a lion in the street."[1] King Solomon, who ruled in Jerusalem three thousand years ago, wrote that about the procrastinator of his day. Thus, we see that this problem runs deep in the human race. Let's consider some of the key *causes* of procrastination.

1ST CAUSE OF PROCRASTINATION: LAZINESS

The biggest cause of procrastination, of course, is laziness. Laziness is by no means a modern problem. Not only did Solomon write about the sluggard with the lame excuse about the lion in the street, he also wrote about the one who puts off even getting up in the morning . . .

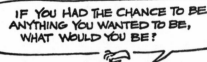

🕐 "As a door turns on its hinges, so a sluggard turns on his bed."[2]

🕐 "Do not love sleep or you will grow poor; stay awake and you will have food to spare."[3]

Solomon's sayings are found in the biblical book of Proverbs, which has a lot to say about laziness. Listen to this ancient wisdom on sloth and the sluggard:

"Go to the ant, you sluggard; consider its ways and be wise! It has no commander, no

© Creators Syndicate, Inc.

> YOUR FRIEND HARV, HAS ALREADY STORED ENOUGH FOOD FOR THE WINTER TO FEED **TWO** FAMILIES.

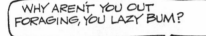

> WHY AREN'T YOU OUT FORAGING, YOU LAZY BUM?

> THAT'S WHAT FRIENDS ARE FOR, DUMMY.

© Creators Syndicate, Inc.

overseer or ruler, yet it stores its provisions in summer and gathers its food at harvest."[4]

Instead of putting off forage and storage, the ant has a lesson for us procrastinators.

What does your boss think of the excessive procrastinator? "As vinegar to the teeth and smoke to the eyes, so is a sluggard to those who send him."[5] What an unpleasant experience to have smoke in your eyes. . . . That's what it's like to our employer when we put off something important!

Proverbs also says, "One who is slack in his work is brother to one who destroys."[6] This underscores the importance of doing our work as if it were for the Lord Himself. Our work should always be of high quality. Years ago, I worked at a gospel radio station, and a woman came to the manager with an album she had recorded with her family. She said, "Now, Dan, when the Lord calls you to do something . . . He doesn't necessarily say, 'Do it well,' He just says, 'Do it.'" My boss told me he knew instinctively it was going to be a *lousy* album, and it was! I like the motto of the church I attend: "Excellence in all things and all things to

God's glory." Excellence in all things is usually not achieved when you put things off to the last minute. Again: "One who is slack in his work is brother to him who destroys."

The Bible also points out, "Whoever watches the wind will not plant; whoever looks at the clouds will not reap."[7] That farmer would do poorly who chooses to only keep

© Creators Syndicate, Inc.

watch of the weather instead of diligently sowing and reaping. "A sluggard does not plow in season; so at harvest time he looks but finds nothing."[8] Many people seem to expect a "harvest" when they have neither sowed nor plowed. The idea that "society" owes it to me or that somehow I'm entitled to have something for nothing is neither consistent with the biblical view of work and labor and rewards, nor with reality. "Sow your seed in the morning, and at evening let not your hands be idle, for you do not know which will succeed, whether this or that, or whether both will do equally well."[9]

"If a man is lazy, the rafters sag; if his hands are idle, the house leaks."[10] A proactive person would use the proverbial "ounce of prevention," and the roof would not get as far as leaking. The procrastinator ends up having more work to do because postponing the matter has made it worse. So we see clearly that laziness is one of the key causes of

procrastination, and we also see this is an age-old problem with time-honored advice on overcoming it. If laziness happens to be your big problem, the most important thing to remember is to simply get started. It doesn't take a rocket scientist to figure out the key to overcoming inertia is to take that first step. We'll cover that in depth in a later chapter.

In the Middle Ages, they classified seven human frailties as the "Seven Deadly Sins." Sloth was one of those seven biggies. Sloth. Laziness. Idleness. The root cause of the bulk of procrastination.

2ND CAUSE OF PROCRASTINATION: AVOIDING PAIN AND SACRIFICE

We often procrastinate because we are trying to avoid something painful or something we just don't want to deal with or view as unpleasant. Motivator Denis Waitley writes,

The culprit is disguised in a six-word slogan: "Relief is just a swallow away." The greatest single cause of what's ailing America, in my opinion, is the "irresponsible obsession with immediate sensual gratification." We want to

© Creators Syndicate, Inc.

love without commitment. We want benefit packages without production requirements. Pain, sacrifice, and effort are unacceptable. If it feels good right away, I'll try it. If I can't be certain to win, then I won't enter. I want the  American Dream I saw on TV, in the movies, and the one my parents said I'd get because I am so special. And I want it now. Tomorrow is too late![11]

That's a fascinating twist on the word *tomorrow*. The procrastinator says about reward: "Give it now;" and about responsibility: "I'll do it tomorrow."

Lee Buck, businessman and author, writes:

I believe there is a diabolical element in human affairs which engenders procrastination. Some simply call it an inner wish to postpone something one doesn't wish to do; others term it a numbing spiritual sickness. I call it a devilish delaying tactic. Yes, I believe in a devil, a spirit of evil with an aim of beguiling humans away from doing good. One of his ploys is to whisper in his victim's ear, "There's plenty of time." It happens when a free lance writer sharpens

© Creators Syndicate, Inc.

pencils instead of sitting at the typewriter, when a housewife turns on the television instead of cleaning her living room, when a student goes out for a hamburger instead of studying for that final exam.

All of them duck the truth that there is *not* plenty of time. The writer never finishes his article, the housewife is too embarrassed to invite guests in, and the student fails his exam.[12]

Is that well put or what?

Another reason for procrastination is that there is something good that we do not wish to give up—at least for now. There is a story about Johannes Brahms going to the doctor, and the doctor told the composer that quite frankly he had to go on a diet. On hearing this, Johannes Brahms smiled and said that of course he would go on the diet, but not today. He couldn't possibly start today because he was dining with Johann Strauss!

Many people would like to change their lives or turn over a new leaf, but not just yet. That reminds me of St. Augustine's classic prayer—Lord, make me chaste . . . but not yet!

People also procrastinate simply because they want to avoid change. Perhaps they could improve their lives significantly just by taking a few steps, but they avoid making changes, so they keep putting things off.

3RD CAUSE OF PROCRASTINATION: THE HABIT OF PROCRASTINATION

Some of us procrastinate from sheer habit. Steven Covey, author of the excellent book, *Seven Habits of Highly Effective People*, says that we need to become more responsible as people. Covey writes:

Look at the word *responsibility*—"response-ability"—the ability to choose your response. Highly proactive people recognize responsibility. They do not blame circumstances, conditions, or conditioning for their behavior. Their behavior is a product of their own conscious choice, based on values, rather than a product of their own conditions, based on feeling.

He goes on to point out that many people by default have allowed themselves to be controlled by outside forces; thus, they become "reactive," as opposed to "proactive." Then Covey goes in for the kill:

> Reactive people are often affected by their physical environment. If the weather is good, they feel good. If it isn't, it affects their attitude and their performance. Proactive people can carry their own weather with them.[13]

That's beautiful! What a great concept, that we can carry our own sunshine with us. If we procrastinate, it's very often because we've developed the habit of procrastinating. Each time we do it, it's like adding thread upon thread. Do it enough, and you end up with many thick strands that are not easily broken. Zig Ziglar, one of my favorite motivational speakers, once said: "Habit is a cable; we weave a thread of it each day until it becomes too strong to break. Then the strength of that habit cable takes us to the top— or ties us to the bottom, depending on whether it is a good habit or a bad one."[14]

Someone once quipped that the largest room in the world is the room for improvement. That may seem corny, but it is true that we often postpone replacing bad habits with good ones for so long that the change never really comes!

Bad habits, like procrastination, can be among the most difficult things to change. Zig Ziglar goes on to say, "When you choose a habit, you also choose the end result of that habit. Good habits are difficult to acquire, but easy to live with."[15] That is *so* true! Zig also says that first you get the habit, and then the habit gets you![16] So choose your habits carefully. It's easy to develop the habit of procrastination—it's what comes naturally! It's difficult to shake the habit, but in the long run, it's worth it.

In many ways, the struggle to stop procrastination is the struggle to control yourself! It's the struggle to discipline yourself. It is a plain matter of self-control. Too often elements in our society play the "blame game," and they blame people and forces outside themselves for their problems. Turn on the TV during the daytime talk shows if you don't believe me. So many of these people never seem to get the point that they are the ones who need to change—even if outside forces *did* do a lot of damage, e.g., dysfunctional parents. Nowadays it seems like everybody's family on TV is dys-

© Creators Syndicate, Inc.

functional! But I've discovered a good solution to that problem. My TV is purposefully dysfunctional during those hours, thanks to the "off" switch!

4TH CAUSE OF PROCRASTINATION: INDECISION (I THINK)

Another cause of procrastination is indecision. People can't decide on a particular course of action. Instead of "yes" or "no," their answer is a definite "maybe." A definite maybe makes it easier to categorize things. It basically means I can decide later . . . maybe!

There's a great promise that I love which addresses indecision. It's a promise from God that if we lack wisdom, all we have to do is ask, and He'll give it! Here's specifically what it says: "If any of you lacks wisdom, he should ask God, who gives generously to all without finding fault, and it will be given to him."[17]

I had an employee when I was in management at a Christian radio station who was from the Deep South, and his accent proclaimed that fact clearly. Whenever you asked him to do something or assigned him a new task, he would agree to it, "Laaawd'-willing." He was alluding to the biblical truth in James that we should not be so cocksure about the future. (We don't know what the future will hold, so while we may make our plans for the future, we will be able to fulfill them only if the Lord wills.[18]) You were always left wondering if perhaps he might be hiding a propensity to procrastinate behind his biblical words. "I'll get to it," he'd reassure us, "Laawd'-willing." Unfortunately, in too many instances, it appeared the Lord wasn't willing!

© Creators Syndicate, Inc.

5TH CAUSE OF PROCRASTINATION: FEAR OF FAILURE

Another major reason people procrastinate is fear, especially the fear of failure. Many people go through life stuck in a dead-end job. They know they should take the necessary steps to improve their lot, to land a better job with a future. But they put it off because they fear that if they try bigger and better things, they might fail. It's true that they might, but even if they do fail, it's a learning experience. Many of life's most successful people were "failures" at one point. How can you succeed at something if you don't give it a shot? Sadly, they put off trying to expand professionally until they are squeezed out in a reorganization or they retire with some modest stipend.

It is not only the fear of failure but *fear* in general that keeps people from doing something that they really would very much like to do.

Some people are so afraid of public speaking that they never say a word in front of any group their whole life. Thankfully, they can join a group like Toastmasters (where you learn public speaking in a safe and friendly atmosphere)—if they get around to it.

© Creators Syndicate, Inc.

Consider the guy in the beginning of the chapter who wouldn't go to work because there was a lion in the street. Now, that probably was only an excuse. But it could also be that he was terrified of lions and that he honestly believed there was one who most certainly would eat him for breakfast. There are many shades of fear, from uneasy feelings to paralyzing phobias, but they can all keep us from doing what we would like or what we think we should do. If a person has a life-dominating phobia, in my view, they ought not put off seeking pastoral or professional help.

CONCLUSION

Procrastination, on the part of two bull-headed young men, turned a beautiful walk into a fatal tragedy. They were on the far northern coast of Scotland. Reportedly there is a road there that is only accessible during low tide. On the left is the sea, and on the right are tall cliffs. One day these two men were idly walking down this road. They were taking in the magnificent sight and oblivious to the danger. At one point, they heard a man shouting from the cliff down to them: "The tide is rising! Behind you and ahead of you the waters have already covered the road. If you go beyond yonder outjutting rock, you'll be swept out to sea. By this ascent alone can you escape!" But they didn't heed his warning. They thought there was a gorge further up by which they could leave the road so they delayed action. But they were wrong, and he was right! Because of their procrastination, these two young men drowned.[19] Whatever the cause of procrastination, in some cases it can have dire consequences.

Chapter 5

© Creators Syndicate, Inc.

"MY NAME IS JERRY AND I'M A RECOVERING PROCRASTINATOR."

One of the greatest labor-saving devices of today is tomorrow.
—Anonymous

There is hope for the procrastinator! I should know. I once was one—and, to some degree, still struggle with it. I think it's important to realize that not only do we procrastinate, but we often make excuses to try and cover it up. So in this

© Creators Syndicate, Inc.

chapter, I want to address the issue of making excuses. I also will talk about my personal battle with this seemingly humorous affliction. If *I* can overcome it as much as I have, anybody can.

EXCUSES, EXCUSES

Every New Year's Day, people turn over new leaves. We make resolutions, and we try to break bad habits. Yet one study found that 70 percent of us have broken our New Year's resolutions by the end of January!

One of the habits many of us try to break is that of procrastination. And with procrastination invariably comes the excuse to try and cover it up. We want to keep a positive self-picture; we want to view ourselves as responsible, diligent, and hard-working.

© Creators Syndicate, Inc.

When we procrastinate, we come across as irresponsible and lazy. We do not like that picture, so we make excuses.

The word *excuse* comes from two Latin words, the prefix *ex* (meaning "away from") and *causa* (meaning "accusation"). "Away from—accusation." To make an excuse is to steer the accusation away from you. Freud seems to have capitalized on this. You can blame all your mistakes, your misdeeds, and the fact that you're a jerk on your mother! To make excuses means to shift the blame from self to others. When we make excuses for procrastination, we simply attempt to mask shoddy workmanship and laziness by shifting the blame from ourselves to others; we simply blame others or outside circumstances for our being late. When we postpone that which we ought to do, we end up cramming a lot of work into an inadequate time slot. The result is less-than-perfect work; hence, the need to find an excuse.

Human beings are great at making excuses. We're great at blaming someone else for our problems. There are some very clever excuses for rationalizing bad behavior. The human mind is a master in self-justification—and people can rationalize just about anything.

EXCUSES FOR PROCRASTINATION

Think of the flimsy excuses you've heard or perhaps have used yourself:
- "But teacher, I can't turn in the assignment today—the dog ate my homework!"
- "Oh, is *that* what you wanted me to do? You weren't clear enough in your instructions."
- "I was going to write that report, but I had to do many other tasks. Besides, you didn't remind me."
- "The computer crashed, and we lost just about all the data." (That's a legitimate problem, but that's why we need to build in time for the unexpected.)
- "I would have been here on time, but I was stuck in traffic."
- "But I was on the phone"—a commonly heard excuse from our teenage daughter for putting off her work.

Note how in each example given, the blame is shifted from the responsible party to someone else. Now if people were honest, they'd tell the real reason they were late in performing some task:

- 🕐 "The remote on the VCR was broken. But VCR Warehouse was closed for the holidays, so I had to drive across town to get it fixed."
- 🕐 "We were having such a good time, I didn't want to stop while it was going strong."
- 🕐 "Everytime I'd look at your memo detailing the report I was supposed to write, I'd cringe. I didn't have a clue how I was supposed to put that thing together."
- 🕐 "How could you expect me to finish this up when the World Series was on?"
- 🕐 "I was snuggled up on the couch with a good cup of coffee, reading a fascinating book. . . . I just couldn't break away."

EXCUSES ARE NOT NEW

This problem of excuses is not a new problem. It goes all the way back to the Garden of Eden. After Adam sinned, did he "fess up"? No way! When God confronted him about it, Adam said, "The woman YOU put here with me—SHE gave me some fruit, and I ate it." And then Eve said, "THE SERPENT deceived me, and I ate." Everybody was blaming somebody else.

Excuses are indeed an old problem and in many ways a spiritual problem.

BELIEF AND BEHAVIOR

One cause of excuse-making is the discrepancy between what we say and what we do. Psychologist L. Festinger came up with the theory of "cognitive dissonance." The theory simply states that people are motivated to achieve consistency between their attitudes and their behavior. If we can't match our theories and beliefs to our behavior we are in dissonance, and if this goes on, over time, serious emotional and mental problems can develop.

A few years ago a politician was pulled over for DWI, driving while intoxicated. The policeman had stopped him because his car was swerving all over the road. When the politician was asked about this, he didn't own up to being drunk. No, he found someone else to blame. When a reporter asked: "Congressman, are you opposed to people drinking and driving?" "Absolutely." "But weren't you drinking and driving?" "No, I wasn't drunk. I was 'overserved.'" We don't want to live with inconsistencies. Either we believe that drinking and driving don't mix and we never do it, or we believe that it's no big deal (or that "I can handle my liquor," etc.). We can't have it both ways.

© Creators Syndicate, Inc.

We have three options when our beliefs and our behaviors don't coincide. First, we—like the congressman—can excuse our behavior. Secondly, we can change our mind and our thinking to fit our behavior, e.g., "These few little drinks aren't going to affect my driving." The third option is to admit that we were wrong and change our behavior. What we cannot do is hold one view while repeatedly contradicting it with our life. How, for example, can a person who has been an atheist all his life explain a sudden interest in God? W. C. Fields, the great comedian, was on his deathbed when a friend came to visit. His friend found him flipping through the Bible. "Bill!" asked his friend, "You're not a religious man. . . . What are you doing reading the Bible?" W. C. Fields answered, "Just looking for loopholes . . . looking for loopholes."

RATS! LATE AGAIN

A common use of excuses is related to time. People fail to be at the right place by the right time, so they try to cover it up with an excuse.

I have often struggled with the habit of being late. I remember many, many years ago finding a good excuse to try to shift blame for my tardiness. If I were about to enter a room where I was late, I would first reset my watch back a few minutes (however many minutes I was late). Then I'd walk in and look and act surprised that I was late. Then I'd look at my watch and then at the clock at the wall, and then I'd shake the watch and listen to it to see if it was still ticking. Then I'd shake my head in disgust and reset the watch to the proper time. I don't know if I ever fooled anybody, especially not when I repeated this charade with the same group!

Here are a couple of interesting stories from the classroom. Some excuses are quite imaginative. *Reader's Digest* tells a true story about a teacher who was handed a note saying, "Dear teacher, please excuse Harriet for missing school yesterday. We forgot to get the Sunday paper off the porch, and when we found it on Monday, we thought it was Sunday."[1]

Another story in *Reader's Digest* happened in an English class. A little boy, the next to the youngest in a family of eight children, arrived totally out of breath. He handed the teacher a note that read, "Please excuse my son's tardiness. I forgot to wake him up, and I did not find him till I started making the beds."[2]

If lack of time is one of your biggest reasons for making excuses for failing to be where you're supposed to be—then just remember this: Everybody has the same amount of time. You decide how to spend it. And,

There's never enough time to do it right.

But there's always enough time to do it over!!!

I remember the first time I got a speeding ticket. It was because I was running so late I missed my train. I was trying to get to work in Chicago, and I was going to take the train from the station at Winnetka, the northern suburb where we lived. But as I pulled up, I saw my train already leaving. So I thought I might be able to catch it in the next town (Kenilworth) or even the next one after that (Wilmette). I caught something else instead—the attention of a policeman! As he pulled me over, and my pulse was racing (I think I earned my weekly thirty aerobic points in that one minute), I pointed out the train to him, and I said, "Do you see that?" He looked over at the train, then looked back at me and said, "Yes." I said, "That's my train." "I see," he said, "May I see your license?"

SNAP IT UP WITH THE DRINKS, MAUDE, THE ICE CUBE IS HERE!

© Creators Syndicate, Inc.

This reminds me of the joke about a speeding motorist who was pulled over by a traffic cop.

> "Going to a fire?" asked the police officer sarcastically.
> "Well, not exactly," said the speeder. "Just trying to prevent one."
> "Yes, and how were you going to do that?"
> "Well, the boss said that's what he'd do if I were late again, and I was hurrying to get to the office in time."[3]

For me, being late has been a symptom of not wanting to waste time by arriving early and just waiting around. So I wasted other people's time instead. The procrastinator times his arrival to make it *just* on time. The problem with that is the unexpected. And the unexpected can alter a fifteen-minute drive into a sixty-minute nightmare of being stuck in gridlock traffic. I heard about an author who was stuck in traffic one day while he was trying to make his way to a radio studio for a live interview. He could hear what the radio host was saying about him, but, not having a cellular phone at that time, he couldn't talk back. I'm sure that was very frustrating.

Being late can't *always* be avoided, but *often* can be—by putting in a little extra time in the schedule, thereby expecting the unexpected! Dr. Richard Swenson, a medical doctor who has witnessed firsthand the devastating effects of stress on our lives, has written about this in his book *Margin: Restoring Emotional, Physical, Financial, and Time Reserves to Overloaded Lives*. Dr. Swenson points out:

> When flying from New York to San Francisco, we don't allow only three minutes to change planes in Denver. A much greater margin of error is needed. But if we make such allowances in our travels, why don't we do it in our living? Life is a journey, but it is not a race. Do yourself a favor

and slow down. . . . God never intended for time to oppress us, dictating our every move.[4]

Not only should we build common sense buffers—Dr. Swenson calls them "margins"—into our schedules, but we should build them into the fabric of our lives.

I used to be late . . . er, that is, I tried to arrive just in time. Take, for example, the airport. It's easier to arrive just in time at the small airports around the country, but that's not the case with larger ones like O'Hare Airport in Chicago (especially during the holidays), as I was to find out one day. I got in deep trouble with my girlfriend, who is now my wife and the coauthor of this book. Being from another country (Norway), she was not as much of a seasoned flier as I was. She had a flight to Arizona to be with some "stateside" relatives. Here was her fiancé-to-be doing his duty to bring her to the airport. How would he do?

Until that date, I always felt it was no big deal to just pull up about fifteen to thirty minutes before the flight—there was plenty of time to spare. But on this particular day, there wasn't. So she missed the flight, and I was responsible. She felt terrible. I think I felt worse. The procrastinator has to pay the consequences for his tardiness.

THE DEVIL MADE ME DO IT

When we are ill-prepared or irresponsible, it's easy to blame someone else. Some people blame all their ills on the devil. The late Flip Wilson struck a nerve several years ago with the slogan, "The devil made me do it!"

This reminds me of the little boy whose mother told him that he absolutely could not go swimming in the river unless she was there. One day he came walking in, soaking wet, with his bathing suit on.

"Johnny, you've been in the river again!"

"But Mama, the devil got behind me and pushed me!"

"Then how is it that you have on your bathing suit?!?"

"Well, I thought he might do that, so I wanted to be prepared."

A CHECKED VICE

Although I have learned to keep procrastination at bay for the most part, the temptation to put things off is still strong. That is why I call it "a checked vice." Sometimes it is possible that we take on more than we can do, just to feed our egos or to please others. On the other hand, I find that the busier I am, the more I can actually get done! (Others have made similar remarks. "If you want to get something done, delegate it to the busy person.") I'm not quite sure why that's the case. I think it's because when you have a lot to do, you get into a no-nonsense mode where you quickly sort out what must be done and what's not important (at the moment).

CONCLUSION

My name is Jerry, and I'm a recovering procrastinator. For the most part, I've shed my excuse-making—covering

© Creators Syndicate, Inc.

up the tendency to put things off. I have learned some lessons along the way that put me in the category of *former* or *recovering* procrastinator.

What has changed me in this realm? Deadlines. Mostly those imposed from without! That is, projects assigned to me that I *had* to do. Even when things seem impossible, I still give it the "old college try," and often, by the grace of God, it works out. And there are several other keys to overcoming procrastination that I've learned through the years. The rest of this book will be dedicated to exploring these.

Part II

SIX KEYS TO OVERCOMING PROCRASTINATION

© Creators Syndicate, Inc.

Chapter 6

© Creators Syndicate, Inc.

PRIORITIZE YOUR PRIORITIES

Put first things first and we get second things thrown in;
put second things first and we lose both first and second things.
—C. S. Lewis

Did you ever hear about the stream-of-consciousness farmer? He went out to tend to the cows, but on his way, he noticed a fence that needed mending. For some time, he had been meaning to get around to fixing it, but he had been putting that off for so long that any big storm could knock it over! So he went into the barn to get his tools. As he entered the workshop portion of his barn where he kept his tools, he saw the mess he had left from the last time he used them. The tools were all over the place, and he started to reorganize them. But then he remembered that he had left the hammer inside the house, so before he finished reorganizing the toolbox, he walked back to the house to get it. On the way to the house, he noticed the four garbage cans that he had not taken out to the street, and he suddenly remembered that this was garbage day! So he hauled two of the garbage cans toward the street, when he noticed the newspaper in the lawn. The headline grabbed his attention, so he went into the house and plopped down in his favorite easy chair—"just for a few minutes"—to read "only" this article. Meanwhile, the cattle were lowing out in the fields.

If there were such a farmer, he would not be in business for long. This dizzying story of how *not* to manage your time brings us to our first key to overcoming procrastination: the importance of priorities. There are so many things to do and so many tasks to choose from and so many good causes to be involved in. The choices we make—or fail to make—determine what we get done.

THE SIX MOST IMPORTANT THINGS TO DO

Early in the twentieth century, Charles Schwab (not the same one of today) managed to turn Bethlehem Steel Company into a major player in that industry in just five years. Mr. Schwab hired efficiency expert Ivy Lee as a consultant to help improve the effectiveness of the company. Lee's advice was both simple and profound. He said that at the end of each day, Charles Schwab and every employee should write out the six most important things that needed to be done during the next work day. And they were to number them in the order of their priority. The next day, each person was to "start on Number One and stay with it until the task was completed; then do Number Two, then Number Three, and so on. It didn't matter if all the tasks were not completed that day. Time was spent on the most important ones."[1] This advice proved to be so effective that Schwab paid Lee $25,000 for it—at a time when $25,000 was a fortune!

I've tried that "six most important things to do today" principle. It's great! Some activities may be contingent on the cooperation of other people. For example, you may have a block in completing Number One because you can't proceed until you have certain vital information from Mr. Smith. Meanwhile, Mr. Smith is not available at the moment. So, you obviously have to move on to Number Two on your list, with an eye to return to Number One later. I mark it "pending" and move on to the next item on my list. But I

© Creators Syndicate, Inc.

make sure I return to it. I may have to re- and re- and return to it. If, after a while, Mr. Smith is still not available, I look for another way to find out that information. Having your itemized, prioritized "To Do" list *on paper* means you can keep referring to it to make sure you're on top of it.

I once read that Dan Rather has a piece of paper that he keeps in his pocket. During the work day, he pulls it out from time to time to read it. It says something to this effect: "Is what you're doing right now contributing toward the broadcast?" This little trick keeps him focused. He has successfully kept a high-pressure, difficult job for a long time! How's that for keeping first things first?

PLANNING FOR THE DAY

The first thing we need to do is think through what we would like to have accomplished by the time the day is done. If we just take the day as it comes, we might leave out important things—until it's too late. Setting aside a few minutes (for me, it works best in the morning; for others, the night before) to plan the day has been a truly helpful habit. It gives me an idea of what really counts for that day.

PRIORITIES AND GOALS

There is an old saying: "If you want to go to heaven, take the road that leads there." This principle is true in all of life. If we want to end up somewhere, there are certain steps that have to be taken in order to make it happen.

Now, in order to make goals for ourselves, we have to establish our priorities first. What's the difference between the two? Priorities are our deep-seated values about what is important to us in life, such as the kingdom of God and our families. Goals are things we want to accomplish or see happen, such as to evangelize or to spend more time with the family. Goals are the outgrowth of our priorities; priorities are the outgrowth of our values. Our values are the outgrowth of our core beliefs. We generally could have about five priorities (e.g., God, family, church, job, social life) whereas we may have fifty goals (say ten goals for each of our priorities).

We should set goals in accordance with our priorities. If the goals we set clash with our priorities, then we experience a natural disharmony. For example, if your priority is to live for God, then it makes no sense to set a goal to become a successful pornographer! That kind of example is obvious.

© Creators Syndicate, Inc.

But here's a more subtle example. If your family is a priority to you and you see that you spend hardly any time at home and seldom see your kids for more than a few minutes at a time, then you know it's time to set some goals to improve your family life.

We need short-term and long-term goals. We need goals for today and goals for a lifetime. We need personal goals and goals for our families. Organizations, businesses, and churches need goals.

Goals can often be encapsulated in a mission statement, in which a person or organization states in one page or even a few words, their purpose and goals. A large firm that provides business products states: "Our mission is to serve our customers as the best supplier of products and services in the markets we serve."[2] A major airline says: "Our vision is for [name of airline] to be the worldwide airline of choice."[3] The mission statement of the great composer Johann Sebastian Bach may have been something to this effect: "I write my music for the enjoyment of the listeners, satisfaction for my supervisors, and the glory of God." Mission statements articulate where we want to go in life.

Meanwhile, we can't do it all, so some things are better left delegated to others. For example . . .

OIL'S WELL THAT ENDS WELL

If you spend a lot of time doing minor repairs on your car that you really don't know how to do, maybe you should hand the car over to a mechanic and use your own time to do what you're better trained to do. The first time I changed my oil was my last! I was changing the oil of my car in my parents' garage. At first, it all seemed to be working fine. I removed the nut, and the old oil began oozing out of the engine into the plastic pan. I went off to do something else while it all drained out. Then I moved the pan out of the way and began to put in the new oil. After having poured in two quarts, it suddenly dawned on me that I didn't recall putting the nut back on. So I looked under the car to check. Sure enough, I hadn't! The garage floor was covered with oil! What a difficult time I had cleaning up all that slimy stuff. I've paid others to change my oil ever since. I know, I know. I could probably save about ten bucks doing it myself. But I don't think that's the best use of my time. It's a high priority for me to make sure the oil in my car gets changed, but it's not a priority that I do it myself.

© Creators Syndicate, Inc.

MUNDANE TASKS THAT MIGHT BE NECESSARY

Many of our daily tasks can often be mundane and sometimes boring, but they are part of what we need to do. This is especially true for housework. Cleaning and maintaining order in a house is very important for all who live there, but it will probably go unnoticed until it's left undone!

Nearly twenty years ago, my wife and I received a large tablecloth for our wedding. It was beautifully embroidered by Kirsti's grandmother. Her grandmother said upon giving it to her, "Please, sew around the edges with your sewing machine so it won't unravel when you wash it." My wife assured her that she would do that. However, seventeen years later it was still not done! Then my wife dreamed that she went to heaven and after a wonderful reunion with Grandma, she asked if the tablecloth had been taken care of. All of a sudden a task for which "there hadn't been time" for seventeen years *instantly* became a priority, and my wife finally got around to doing it.

The important things in life are often quite simple. Consider some examples: spending time with God, visiting with family and friends, taking time to read to our children or talk to our spouse, taking time for exercise, making a phone call to a friend to see how they are, making someone's day special, spending time with our immediate family, spending time with your spouse, writing a letter or sending a friend an E-mail. In short, *relationships* are among the most important, yet least urgent, things for us to not put off. Part of the reason that there is such a meltdown in our society is because of the meltdown in relationships. Too often if people don't get along with their friends, coworkers, or even spouses, they just trade in their old ones for new ones! Then they wonder why their lives lack continuity and stability.

Here are some priorities that people are pursuing. Which five are most important to you? What others would you add to the list?

- 🕐 Follow God's will.
- 🕐 Stay close to my wife/husband.

© Creators Syndicate, Inc.

- 🕐 Achieve financial security.
- 🕐 Rear our children properly.
- 🕐 Spend time with the kids.
- 🕐 Attend church regularly.
- 🕐 Be involved in church work.
- 🕐 Be a good son/daughter.
- 🕐 Spend time with my parents.
- 🕐 Develop strong and lasting friendships.
- 🕐 Advance in my career.
- 🕐 Be the best in my field.
- 🕐 Always look my best.
- 🕐 Create the best home possible.
- 🕐 Find an interesting hobby.
- 🕐 Visit different countries.

And on and on.

SPIRITUAL PRIORITIES

Sometimes it may seem hard to figure out our spiritual priorities. An intriguing little story in the gospel challenges conventional wisdom on this front. This story is in Luke, and it involves two sisters, Mary and Martha. It says that Martha and Mary opened their home to Jesus. Martha was taking care of all the details—she was cooking and setting the table and arranging for the Master's stay, while Mary sat at His feet and just listened to Him speak. Martha got fed up with her sister just sitting there as if there was nothing to be done! As a matter of fact, she got so upset that she went to Jesus and said: "Lord, don't you care that my sister has left me to do all the work by myself? Tell her to help me!" You would think the Lord would have told Mary to get in there and help her sister, but no! He told Martha that while she was worried and upset about so many things, there was only one thing that was important. He said that Mary had chosen what's better, and it would not be taken from her. What was it that was so important? It was listening to the word of the Master. Martha was caught up in the urgent tasks. Mary had chosen the important one—paying heed to the word of God.[4]

As Christians we are to have a daily time with God, reading the Bible and praying. When we pray for help and direction and guidance in our day, we find that our priorities come into focus and we see what's important. Jesus said, "Seek first the kingdom of God and His righteousness, and all these things [things that you need] shall be added unto you"[5] (author's addition). When we seek God—His kingdom, His work, His priorities—then all the other things of life fall into place.

I believe we are put here on earth for God's glory and for the benefit of our fellow man. When General William Booth, the founder of the Salvation Army, died, he left his followers with one word to help and guide them and that word was *others*. In this word you can find the key to fulfilling work and a lifetime of happiness. When a person works for his own happiness, it often eludes him, but when we give of ourselves and work for others,

© Creators Syndicate, Inc.

something amazing happens: We often get all the other things thrown in. We might not get all the toys, like the latest car or high-powered motor boats, but we experience a deep abiding contentment with life that often escapes those who may be fabulously wealthy.

The important things in life, the ones we should not leave undone, often don't seem urgent. Barbara Bush once addressed the graduating class of Wellesley College and reminded them of the importance of investing in relationships:

> At the end of your life, you will never regret not having passed one more test, not winning one more verdict, or not closing one more deal. You will regret time not spent with a husband, a friend, a child, or a parent.[6]

THE OBITUARY TEST

So, let's take a moment to think through our priorities and goals. What are *your* goals? What do you want to achieve in life?

Have you ever heard of the obituary test? It's when you think of the end of your life and work backwards. How do you want your obituary to read? What do you *really* want to have accomplished by the time you breathe your last? If you don't like to think about your obituary, here is a more fun idea. Pretend you have just retired. Talk to your spouse (or a friend) about your life—what you have done, all the places you went to, and all the things you accomplished, the people you have known, and what you would like the rest of your life to be like. This'll give you a good look at what you really want out of life.

Think about what you want to do and what priorities you already have. Some things that you have considered important might not be that important after all. On the other hand, there might be things that should have a higher priority than they have right now.

Take a moment to list your own priorities in life:

1. _____   2. _____

3. _____   4. _____

5. _____   6. _____

After that is done, take another moment and think about your goals. What kind of things follow from your priority list? Jot down as many things as come to mind in the course of a couple of minutes. For example, if one of my priorities is to spend more time with my children, what kind of goals should I set to accomplish this? It could be:

- 🕐 Free up some time each day.
- 🕐 Get a book of attractions in our area.
- 🕐 Get bikes for the whole family.
- 🕐 Get some board games.
- 🕐 Read aloud.
- 🕐 Plan specific activities with the family.

Now list a few goals to fit one of your priorities:

_____

_____

_____

_____

_____

Now compare the two lists (priorities and goals) just to make sure there are no conflicts.

Go through the list of goals and put a number on the side to prioritize them. If you could only do one of those things, which one would it be? Write a 1 by that item. Then choose number two, and write a 2 by that item, etc. If you want, write these on a separate piece of paper in the ascending order of priority and review them as often as you wish—daily, weekly, monthly. It's good to remind yourself of what your goals are. If you're really ambitious, you could create lots of goals for each of your priorities.

SEASONS IN LIFE

Keep in mind as you think through your priorities and goals that there are seasons in life. For example, when we are involved in rearing children, that is our priority. Or maybe you have been called to take care of a sick relative or elderly parents. These seasonal tasks may seem of little significance, but they often have bigger consequences we can't always see.

Also remember that the job you have might not be everything you had wished for, but if it provides for your family and gives you honest wages, then it is good and right. It might not be your ideal job, yet it may still be moving you

© Creators Syndicate, Inc.

toward that ideal job (provided it's not a "dead-end job"). Your job might not be an end in itself, but the means by which you fulfill your priority of caring for your own. Of course, if you don't like anything about it and you are unhappy every day, it might be time to look for something better.

WHAT REALLY MATTERS IN LIFE

Some people see life as pretty meaningless, and all they wish to do is have as much fun as possible, like the Epicureans of ancient times. If one task is just as good as another, it doesn't matter what we do.

On the other hand, if you believe (as we do) that our lives have eternal significance and that what we do, say, and think has consequences for both time and eternity, then everything is put into a different perspective, and priorities become of utmost importance.

Personally, I like a phrase from the Mayflower Compact as a purpose for life. The Pilgrims said they came on the voyage "for the glory of God and the advancement of the Christian faith." For me, this is a great summary of the purpose of my life. What's your purpose? I want to hear Jesus say to me at the end of my life, "Well done, thou good and faithful servant." To hear those words will make any temporary deprivations or sacrifices in this life all worthwhile!

© Creators Syndicate, Inc.

CONCLUSION

When we know what we ought to do, what we want to do, and why it is important for us to do these things, we have taken a giant step toward a life of overcoming procrastination. As Mr. Anonymous once put it:

> Better try to do something
> And fail in the deed
> Than try to do nothing
> And always succeed.[7]

So, please think for a moment, and write down those six most important items for you to do tomorrow (or today), then, number them in the order of their priority. Do Number One until it's finished. Then Number Two. Try this at least for a week, and I'll bet you'll already begin to see procrastination falling by the wayside! You'll be way ahead of the game compared to our hypothetical farmer, who, by the way, was last heard of driving to the feed store, but, on his way, he noticed. . . .

Chapter 7

© Creators Syndicate, Inc.

HOW TO EAT AN ELEPHANT

If you want to make an easy job seem mighty hard, just keep putting off doing it.
—Olin Miller

Why do we procrastinate? We put off tasks for so long that they begin to look too big to handle. Then we want to put them off even more! I read about a fitness author who at one point earlier in her life was significantly overweight. She says, "The first time I tried an aerobic class, when I was 260 pounds, I left in tears. All those thin gorgeous women in fabulous workout clothes—doing exercises that

my body couldn't do at that weight."[1] She didn't gain that weight overnight, and she wasn't about to lose it overnight. But eventually she was able to set smaller goals that she was able to achieve, and she ended up shedding 130 pounds.

Eating an elephant seems virtually impossible. So how *do* you eat one? One bite at a time. We often put off tasks because they seem formidable; however, when we break them down into smaller parts, we can get virtually anything done. The time-honored principle of divide and conquer will work wonders for the procrastinator who wants to reform.

ATOMS AND MOLECULES, PARAGRAPHS AND SENTENCES, WORDS AND LETTERS

Everything in our world can be broken down into parts. All parts can be broken down into atoms and molecules. Our bodies are made of tiny cells. Every book can be broken down into chapters, pages, and paragraphs. Paragraphs can be broken down into sentences and words. And words can even be broken down into letters. The whole is the sum of its parts.

And in the same way, every task, no matter how complex, can be reduced to a series of steps. Every task. The key, then, to this aspect of overcoming procrastination is to break tasks down into minitasks. It's really only when we try to do it *all at once* that we get frustrated because it generally can't be done all at once.

The old cliché is true: It's a trial by the mile, but a cinch by the inch.

If you have to do something but you've been putting it off, instead of constantly procrastinating, think about it in terms of what steps—or ministeps—need to be taken to accomplish it. Let the first step be making a list. Then you do each item on the list, one at a time. That's how you eat an elephant, one bite at a time.

EXAMPLES OF DIVIDING AND CONQUERING

Let's consider some examples of applying this principle. Suppose you've been putting off something as simple as an unpleasant phone call. You could divide this task into several little tasks you can do one at a time. Let's see. Here are steps you could take:

1. Look up the phone number.
2. Set aside an appointed time when you'll make the phone call.
3. Get out the file and review the situation.
4. Decide exactly what you plan to say.
5. At the appointed time, place the call.[2]

It's that simple. Of course, the serious procrastinator may add a few more steps at various stages of this assignment—such as . . .

- ⏲ Look around for the phone book,
- ⏲ Sharpen your pencil to jot down the number,
- ⏲ Warm up the phone by calling your best friend, etc.

Let's use a tougher example. Suppose you've been putting off writing a ten-page report for work. The first step is to thoroughly review the assignment and decide who should actually write the report. A lot of things that we think we need to do, we don't. Either it doesn't need to be done or we can legitimately pass it on to someone else. There's a time and a place to delegate. Even with delegation, you can break that down to several mini-tasks, such as: 1) Make an appointment with the person to whom you're delegating the task; 2) At the appointed time, sit down with them and go over the details; 3) Coordinate plans for follow up and review.

Let's assume after thinking it through, you determine it is *your* responsibility to write this report. Then take a moment to consider how this can be broken down into easy-to-accomplish tasks. You may need to do some research for it. You may need to delegate *part* of it to be written by someone else. You may need to have some charts or other visual aids made for it. You need to write an outline, and then, of course, write the report. But break it down even further. Let's suppose there will be roughly five parts to this report, and three of them deal with material you know so well you could probably write them off the top of your head. Let's suppose you need to do a fair amount of research before you can write the other two parts. And further, let's suppose that one of those parts could be delegated to someone else to research and write—if you can get them to do this within your time limits. Now, make a list of what needs to be done.

Let's see . . .

- Write an outline for the whole thing.
- Write an outline for part one.
- Write part one.
- Write an outline for part two.
- Write part two.
- Delegate part three to Gail (if she has the time. If she doesn't, she needs to give some input so you can write it.)
- Write an outline for part four.
- Write part four.
- Research part five.
- Write an outline for part five.
- Write part five.
- Have someone make charts for the whole report (or generate them yourself on your computer).

- ⏲ Assemble all these parts together.
- ⏲ Spellcheck them.
- ⏲ Reread and tweak the whole thing.
- ⏲ Make the title page.
- ⏲ Possibly have someone else go over it when it's finished. Then you can make appropriate changes.

After writing these various component parts, I suggest you then place a number by these ministeps in the order you plan to do them (starting with the easiest task first— we'll see why in the momentum chapter). In the case where you need to delegate things to others (e.g., part three or the graphics), list them first or thereabouts so that others can be working on their part while you are working on yours. That way work on different parts of this report will go on simultaneously.

Using the steps above as an example, here's how you might prioritize them:

1. Write an outline for the whole thing.
2. Write an outline for part one.
3. Write part one.
4. Write an outline for part two.
5. Write part two.
6. Delegate part three to Gail.

© Creators Syndicate, Inc.

7. Write an outline for part four.
8. Write part four.
9. Research part five.
10. Write an outline for part five.
11. Write part five.
12. Have someone make charts for the whole report.
13. Assemble all these parts together.
14. Spell check them.
15. Reread and touch up the whole thing.
16. Make the title page.
17. Have Person B read the whole thing.
18. You then tweak the report with those suggestions in mind.

After making this list and ordering the priority of it all, then do #1 and check it off, do #2 and check it off, etc. If you get interrupted or feel that you should switch the order of some of these steps while the project is in process, fine. Just keep at it until you're finished with the whole thing. The time-honored principle of divide and conquer will work wonders for the procrastinator who wants to reform.

Is it really worth taking the time to break these assignments down? Not if you will do them on time and not put them off. But if you tend to put things

© Creators Syndicate, Inc.

© Creators Syndicate, Inc.

off, then it's definitely worth it, because it helps you to see that what you've been putting off isn't so difficult after all. Often the reason things get to be so difficult is that the day comes when you finally *have* to do it. By then, the task *is* formidable! Who knows? You may have to stay up all night to get it all done!

Even if you can't finish *all* of a given task (because something is pending), you can still work on many of the steps. Then when that thing you've been waiting for comes, you can handle it at that time.

Surely by now you get the hang of all this. So . . .

WHAT HAVE *YOU* BEEN PUTTING OFF?

Take a moment to consider what you've been putting off. How can you divide that particular task into ministeps? Even if some of them may seem like ridiculous baby steps, so what? First of all, list one task you've been putting off that you really want to get around to some day: _____

_____.

OK. Now, how many ministeps—no matter how absurd—can you divide that task into?

_____

_____

_____

_____

_____

_____

_____

_____

_____

_____

_____

_____

Now, look at the task. Look at the ministeps. Doesn't the task lose its formidableness in light of all these little steps?

It's good to go ahead and take one of these steps. Complete it today if you can. Then reward yourself! Congratulate yourself for having taken a step, no matter how small, toward completion. You've been putting this task off perhaps for days, weeks, months, years, and now you've made a step (no matter how small) toward its completion.

Motivational speaker Barbara Sher once pointed out that there are two key steps to overcoming resistance, as in resistance to doing what you know you should be doing. First, commit to doing something so small that you'll do it at least once a day, every day. Thus, break down the goal into a small part—a teeny-weeny part! For instance, if the goal involves exercise and deals with sit-ups as an example (and this is her example), and you've been experiencing resistance in this area, then commit to doing at least *one* sit-up a day. If on a day you don't feel like it, then at least knowingly refuse to do it that particular day. Secondly, find at least one thing you love about it. For example, suppose you enjoy feeling your muscles tense as you do that one sit-up, then focus on that. There is no question that virtually the hardest part of any task is just getting started. So if it takes that little of a commitment to get going, by all means do it. You can't do everything to change the world—or even to change your world—but you can do something, no matter how small it might be. This is the how-to-eat-an-elephant principle taken to the nth degree.

CONCLUSION

Have you ever had that feeling of *dread* that comes from putting something off that you should have done a long time ago? Then, every time you see some reminder of it, the guilt feeling returns because you know you've been procrastinating? It kind of hangs over you like the Sword of Damocles

© Creators Syndicate, Inc.

(whatever that was). Do yourself a favor—the next time that happens, take a few minutes and jot down as many potential steps as you can think of to complete that formidable task. Suddenly, it will lose its power of control over you. What was unmanageable becomes manageable, and you'll be eating elephant hors d'oeuvres before you know it! Mmmmmm.

Chapter 8

© Creators Syndicate, Inc.

BUILD MOMENTUM

We cannot do everything at once, but we can do something at once.
—Calvin Coolidge

M any years ago, I was part of a missions group. We were driving up the side of a mountain in the Andes on an unpaved road. At one point, the mud was so bad that the car got bogged down, and we all had to get out and do everything we could to keep it going. Once we lost momentum, it took a long time to negotiate that long patch of mud mistaken for a road. We had to go around and find rocks to put in the tires' paths. We had to push and shove, to rock the car back and forth. It was a mess. Even though this stretch of road wasn't that long, the mud had us bogged down for at least an hour. It was hard work to keep the car moving. There was no option but to keep going; we had to reach our goal before the sun went down. Fortunately, someone came down from the top of the mountain and helped us with his shovel. Because we had no choice, because we had to keep going, because of the man's skill with the shovel, we prevailed. But how many projects in life get abandoned after we hit the patches of mud? The key point of this chapter is to build up momentum and to keep it going. Since the hardest part of any job is to get started, then to overcome procrastination: 1) get started, and 2) keep going!

A LESSON FROM STONEWALL JACKSON

I have learned a great lesson from Stonewall Jackson, one of America's greatest military leaders. Jackson accomplished some unbelievable feats in his day.[1] For example, in the Shenandoah campaign of 1862, he had an army of approximately 17,500. They certainly had far fewer resources (food, clothing, shoes, ammunition) than their Northern counterparts, but to the victors belong the spoils! With these brave and well-trained men (some of whom were barefoot) and with a better knowledge of the terrain than his opponents, Jackson beat an army that was roughly ten times bigger!!! That's staggering when you think about it. How did he do it? The secret should be of interest to procrastinators the world over. He seized the momentum and never let go.

When facing an opponent, Jackson's army would look for the weakest link they could find at the moment. They would tenaciously go after that flank or that section until it was defeated. Then they would go to the next one until it too was vanquished. They would keep this up until victory was complete! Jackson himself said, "Always mystify, mislead, and surprise the enemy. And when you strike and

© Creators Syndicate, Inc.

overcome him, never let up in the pursuit. Never fight against heavy odds if you can hold your force on only a part of your enemy and crush it. A small army may thus destroy a large one and repeated victory will make it invincible."[2]

Picture the poor Union forces going up against Stonewall's well-organized and highly disciplined soldiers. It would have been a strange sight to see his men defeat a much larger army of men who were better-fed and better-clothed but weren't as well organized. Stonewall's men would generally take advantage of any slowdown on the part of the Federal soldiers. One time, Alexander the Great was asked how he had conquered the world. His answer? "By not delaying."[3] Build up momentum, and you begin conquering a defeatist attitude.

© Creators Syndicate, Inc.

So how does this relate to overcoming procrastination? It boils down to this: Do what's easiest to do first. Then when you've finished that, do the next easiest. And keep going until you're finished. Once you've got the momentum, you can get all sorts of things done. And it all gets back to the realization that the hardest part of any task is getting started.

In the last chapter, we learned to divide tasks into minitasks. Now we're discussing the *order* in which to complete those minitasks. When I say do the easiest first, implied in that is this context: *assuming the priority of all those minitasks is equal.* That's an important caveat! Otherwise, one may end up doing something easy that's irrelevant to the overall picture. That's like doing a "stove job" as we discussed in chapter 1. Thus, the momentum principle I'm describing here deals with a multitude of equally important minitasks that make up the whole assignment.

REAL LIFE EXAMPLES

For five years, I worked part-time at the Miami affiliate of the Home Shopping Club. Wanna buy a ring? Honk, honk. No, actually, I didn't sell anything. Instead, I helped keep the station legal with the FCC. I produced, hosted, and edited little four-and-one-half-minute public affairs features that had nothing to do with the shopping. These features ran every hour. Once a month, it was my custom to go in early on a Saturday morning and do a marathon editing shift to put together four or five six-part series of these segments. This was a lot of work, and if I had worked there 9 to 5 during the weekdays, it may well have taken at least two, maybe even three or more days, given the normal interruptions. Yet I would usually come in about five or six o'clock and work until midnight, and be finished with a month's worth of my quota of these segments! How? By applying this Stonewall Jackson principle. I'd determine which was easiest and could be done first. Then I'd sit down and edit that series. Then I'd do the next easiest, etc. Thus, segment by segment, a series was edited, and then series by series, the work would be completed. By the time I got to the fourth or fifth series (which may have been much trickier and may have required a lot more editing), I would have been so revved up that I would just keep going. Usually by the time midnight or so rolled around, I would have finished what would normally take more than eighteen hours.

When I work on a book, I use the Stonewall Jackson principle to tackle the assignment. I don't necessarily write chapter one first. I don't necessarily write the second chapter first. I write that which is easiest first, then that which is second easiest, and so on, until it's all done. This principle has served so well because when you get bogged down and delayed, it's easy to want to procrastinate.

Even when writing the chapters themselves, I may get bogged down in a certain section and create delays. So what I try to do now is to simply type in all caps something I'll write later (but can't think of now). This way I can keep going, and get "the big Mo" (momentum) working for me. For example, I always try to lead off each chapter with an interesting story, some little tidbit to grab the reader's attention. But if I'm sitting down to write a new chapter, and I can't think of one right away, I'll simply type: OPENING ANECDOTE and then I'll proceed with the text that does come to mind. If, after a few pages, I come to a portion that may require some research or may require some book or article

or item I don't have available to me right then and there, I'll type that topic name in all caps (let's say the topic is Lincoln's second inaugural address) and then I'll type the title and what I need to do with it, e.g.:

LINCOLN'S SECOND INAUGURAL—READ AND QUOTE ONE OR TWO LINES

Then I'll keep going. I might not be able to do it all, but I do what I can and keep going. This is similar

© Creators Syndicate, Inc.

to someone taking a test who comes to a question to which they don't immediately know the answer and skipping on to the next question, with the plan that they'll try that one later. Usually, if you know the material, when you do come back to that question—after having built up momentum—you're able to return to it and get it right (or at least give an intelligent guess).

I produce a lot of documentaries for Coral Ridge Ministries. This too is broken up into several parts. Once I've finished with the field production and decided what the overall sections will be, then I plow into that which I can complete first, even if it happens to be the last segment of the whole program.

Momentum, momentum, momentum.

Momentum helps overcome that initial phase where it's hard to get started. Here's advice from Lee Buck, a successful businessman: "When I feel reluctant to get going in a job, I force myself to do something, anything, as long as it's part of the task. The very doing is resisting the devil, or sloth, whatever you may wish to call the problem. And it is not long before it fades or 'flees' from you."[4]

© Creators Syndicate, Inc.   2·17

AN INVISIBLE LINE

Somewhere in the middle of a project, there's an invisible line from dread to joy. Even if you've been putting this project off, once you get going with it and you have a good handle on it, you go from hating it or fearing it to enjoying it. At least I do. I don't know where that invisible line is or even if you will always cross it. After all, some things that we have to do may be unpleasant every step along the way. But for me, no matter what the project is, once I'm actually "cooking," once I'm going "full throttle," once I'm hitting "pay dirt" (you name the cliché!), then I start to enjoy the process.

When I'm in that full throttle mode, then I often find interruptions difficult. In fact, when I'm in certain phases of "post-production" at work, where I'm doing the creative editing of an hour-long documentary, story by story or section by section, I often do something we have available at work. I program my phone so it won't ring, but the caller will immediately be sent into voice mail. Obviously, not everyone has the luxury to do that. I find it so productive to work in uninterrupted blocks of time. When you get sidetracked on a project, it may take some time to build up steam again. Again, this all gets back to momentum.

A HUNDRED-YEAR DELAY

Here's an intriguing example of a sidetrack that lasted quite a long time! Years ago I had the privilege of sightseeing in Switzerland. One of the most interesting things I saw was a large church with two bell towers, one on each side of the front (roughly the way Notre Dame is designed). However, the towers of this medieval cathedral were very different from each other. They weren't symmetrical carbon copies of each other. My tour guide told me that this was because in the course of building the beautiful edifice, they had run out of money. So the original builders had constructed one of the bell towers, but not the other. It was not until a hundred years later that the other tower was completed. However, by then, everyone involved in the original construction had long since died and apparently there were no blueprints to be found. So rather than trying to create an equal opposite, the new builders created their own design. What I find interesting about this story is that the initial momentum of building that cathedral got bogged down so completely that there was a hundred-year delay in finishing the project. Once you get stalled

© Creators Syndicate, Inc.

in a project, it's easy to put it on a back burner unless you absolutely have to do it.

CONCLUSION

Elisabeth Elliot in her book on finding God's will, *A Slow and Certain Light*, writes: "Some duty lies on my doorstep right now. It may be a simple thing which I have known for a long time I ought to do, but it has been easy to avoid. It is probably the thing that springs to my mind when I pray the prayer, 'We have left undone those thing we ought to have done.'"[5] Is there some project that makes you feel guilty because you've been putting it off? Well, instead of wallowing in guilt or shutting your mind to it, take these simple steps: Break it all down to small parts—perhaps as many as you can. Then prioritize those parts. If all things are equal as far as the priorities are concerned, then do the easiest to finish first, then the next easiest, and keep going until you're done! It's so important to seize the momentum and not let it go.

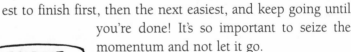

© Creators Syndicate, Inc.

Chapter 9

© Creators Syndicate, Inc.

BRING PROJECTS TO LIFE WITH DEADLINES

Never put off until tomorrow what you can do
the day after tomorrow just as well.
—Mark Twain

One time someone asked the head of a successful business what it took to get started. His answer should be helpful to procrastinators everywhere. He said, "a sense of urgency about getting things done." An inspirational and motivational magazine commenting on that president's remark said, "The people who make things move in this world share this same urgency. . . . The world is full of very competent people, who honestly intend to do things tomorrow, or as soon as they can get around to it. Their accomplishments, however, seldom

© Creators Syndicate, Inc.

match those of less-talented people who are blessed with a sense of the importance of getting started now. Do it now!!"[1]

There's a secret word that brings unusual power to the subject of procrastination. The word is *deadline*. I'm surprised at what can be accomplished when a monumental deadline stands before me. It may seem unrealistic. It may seem outrageous. But I'm amazed how many times I've met such deadlines. I find that I accomplish much more through difficult (but not impossible) deadlines.

We are capable of achieving much more than we do. Deadlines help push us to greater achievement. Let's explore how deadlines can nip procrastination in the bud.

WORK EXPANDS TO THE TIME ALLOTTED

Have you ever heard of Parkinson's Law? According to Edwin Bliss in his book *Getting Things Done,* Parkinson's Law states that "work expands to fill the time available for its completion." Therefore, points out Bliss, "make less time available for a given task and you will get it done more quickly."[2]

I've seen people take forty to fifty hours to accomplish something that only takes someone else ten to fifteen hours! Obviously, other factors are involved, but one of the keys is that the quicker employee allowed himself less time to achieve his objective. And his output was essentially as good as the others!

I remember one summer after I graduated from college I decided to take the entire summer off "to get organized." During that time I accomplished very few things. Very few. It was an "in between" type of time. I did decide to go to graduate school, which I had already been considering. I did spend some time with a volunteer program, visiting a juvenile delinquent on a regular basis. And I spent a few weekends helping a friend by loading film for a 16mm motion picture documentary he was making. And I relaxed a bit. What else did I accomplish? Let's see . . . I got caught up on my correspondence. I gave blood. I took my GRE's. That was about it. That was about all I can show for three months of my adult life. Always before that, and after it, I worked during the summer. But the summer of '78 I took off just to "get caught up with myself," and I never seemed to reach that elusive objective. I remember one friend telling me over and over during that time, "Get your act together!" What was missing from this period of zip achievement? Motivation, goals, and *deadlines*.

© Creators Syndicate, Inc.

When you have a deadline—a realistic but *challenging* deadline—it energizes you to strive to achieve what you may never have thought possible. Show me an activity that you're going to do one of these days "when you get around to it," and I'll show you something you may well put off ad infinitum. If you decide something is important, then give yourself a deadline—a realistic but challenging one. Make it difficult, but attainable. Furthermore, you can always give deadlines not only for major tasks but for minitasks as well.

Deadlines given at work often cause a lot to get done. I do think that balance is needed here though. It is true that some people make all their strenuous deadlines, and then they drop dead of a heart attack without really enjoying the fruits of their labor. What good is that?

ORIGIN OF THE WORD "DEADLINE"

Originally a deadline meant a line drawn in the dirt or sand in a prison that an inmate went beyond *only* at the risk of being shot. The word *deadline* was born in the notorious Confederate prison of Andersonville, Georgia. Tony Horwitz writes: "There were . . . posts delineating the 'deadline,' a perimeter inside the stockade that no prisoner could cross without risking gunfire from the guard towers."[3] It's amazing that what was once associated with death and misery is really something that can now give birth and life to a project.

REALISTIC DEADLINES

A realistic but challenging deadline is a true energizer. It can motivate you. It can get you ready to diligently go about the task at hand like nothing else.

It's important that deadlines be realistic. It can be self-defeating to consistently set goals and consistently miss the deadlines! I wonder if it's better to not even set the goal in the first place. I know what this trap is like. I've often gone through a merry-go-round of dieting. I have too often made weight-loss goals that were so unrealistic that I essentially set myself up for failure. I couldn't lose weight by those deadlines I gave myself even if I used all the diets in *National Enquirer*. e.g. "Lose 30 pounds in 30 days!" Not achieving those unrealistic goals then made me feel bad—but nothing that malted milk balls couldn't remedy! So, when it's all said and done, internal deadlines will only work if they're *realistic*.

The best way to determine the deadline is to think through realistically what it will take to achieve the goal in question and then subtract a little time from that amount—just to give yourself an extra push. It's like jumping into the freezing waters of a cold pool. It awakens the whole body. Every fiber of your being gets stimulated and wide awake. If you were tired or groggy before, no longer! So it is with a realistic, but challenging, deadline. It is an energizer.

If you're self-employed or your deadlines are internal, I suggest you confide in a friend, someone you can trust, someone you know who wants the best for you. Share with him or her your goal and the deadline for its achievement. Have him or her keep you accountable for your goal. But let that person be an *encourager* and not a bully (someone who enjoys beating you down for the slightest infraction from your objective) or an enabler (who will commiserate with you as to why you didn't achieve your deadline). In short, accountability with someone else—the

right person—can help make the internal deadlines more realistic to achieve. We'll have more to say about accountability in a later chapter.

Think of a deadline as an opportunity to compete against yourself, not somebody else. If the goal is to achieve XYZ by September 1, why not try to have it finished by August 30 or 15 or 1? It's fun to work on these things and challenge yourself to a higher output than you're used to.

© Creators Syndicate, Inc.

MY FIRST BOOK PROJECT

When I worked on my first book project (before I learned that the wheels of publishing grind slooooooooooooooooowly), I couldn't *believe* the publisher's deadline. From my perspective, the publisher had seemingly dragged out the process for month after anxious month. Finally, a representative of the publisher told me around Thanksgiving time that they had accepted the book, and he asked me when I could have the manuscript ready. I guesstimated by early August. But after a few weeks, no contract came forth. A few weeks soon turned into a few months and still no contract. I worked on the book off and on—but more off than on. I was beginning to wonder if the project would *ever* come to fruition. It finally did—on March 10. I'll never forget the date.

I was so pleased and elated, but one little detail blew me away. They wanted the manuscript completely finished by August 1! "You want it when? Ha Ha Ha." I called someone to ask about the deadline. He told me that that date was *binding*. No manuscript by August 1, no contract. But, but, but . . . I didn't see how I could possibly make this deadline!

Well, as can be guessed, I made the deadline. I devised for myself a series of mini-deadlines. I opened the calendar and plotted out a deadline for the completion of at least the first working rough draft of each chapter. (Basically, several Saturdays served as my due dates.) And I met the deadlines, week after week, because I *had* to. I applied all the strategies we've discussed so far: the divide and conquer principle; the key of ordering each step in the order of priority; the Stonewall Jackson principle (I did the easiest to complete first); challenging, but realistic, deadlines for each chapter. I also built in time for tweaking the book and having it reviewed by a friend. And, by the grace of God, I got it done . . . and on time. Deadlines were the key.

ACCOMPLISHMENT VS. ACTIVITY

Activity is not the same as accomplishment. A paper shuffler could be busy for eight hours and accomplish nothing. Did you ever hear about processionary caterpillars that walk around and around the pot following the caterpillars right in front of them? Once an experimenter placed several of these on the rim of a flower pot. He also placed food inside the pot, yet those critters kept following the leader (whoever that was!) who was following the last one in the line. So this circle of caterpillars went round and round until they literally dropped dead from lack of food, yet food was available only inches away. What a striking picture of *activity* without accomplishment. I don't ever want to be like those processionary caterpillars. I want my life to count for something.

Many people seem to go through life virtually marking time. They could just as well be in prison marking the days as they go by. They're not using their liberty for anything worthwhile.

Many people plan a great deal for the weekend or for the annual vacation, but they do very little planning for their lives, for their future, for all their "everydays."

© Creators Syndicate, Inc.

Without deadlines, sometimes we can end up in dead-end routines. Many people continue for years in jobs where there's no real hope for change in sight. Chances are whoever you are, whatever your level of education, you can fit somewhere in the economy to provide a better service for others, which in turn will generally cause you to earn more money. But it isn't helpful to put off addressing this.[4]

If you are stuck in a rut, consider asking a relative or family member for short-term help so you may take some intermediate steps to better yourself. Consider taking on a part-time job on the weekends that will help lead you in the direction you want to go. There are a multitude of adult educational opportunities available. I suggest beginning with an aptitude test. These are available—often for free or a minimal fee—at your local community college. Such a test can help you pinpoint a career where you would be strong and can help identify areas of interest. Another thing relatives or friends (or a healthy savings account) might help you with is freeing you to take a nonpaying internship in your chosen field of interest. An effective internship at the right place can give you invaluable experience and break through this well-known "catch-22": You can't get a job until you have experience, and you can't get experience until you've had a job! The solution is to get experience through an internship, through volunteer work, through a part-time job on weekends, through any way you can legally get it. If you're a college student, don't just go

© Creators Syndicate, Inc.

after good grades, go after extracurricular activities in your chosen field. They may mean more on your résumé to prospective future employers than your GPA!

People generally do best what they love. What do you enjoy doing? What are you gifted at? What are you interested in? Remember the slogan and book title: *Do What You Love and the Money Will Follow?* There's a lot of truth to that.

If you're stuck in a professional rut, create a realistic but challenging deadline for finding a new position or for improving your lot.[5] Here are two easy, arbitrary deadlines to give yourself: Christmas or summer. Try and get that new promotion or new job by Christmas or by the summer (depending on when you create the deadline and how long it will take). And stick with it, even if you receive repeated rejection.

Cartoonist Johnny Hart, whose work graces these pages, provides a great example of how persistence with or without deadlines pays off. In the 1950s, he was gainfully employed by GE, but his real interest was in drawing pictures. Inspired by the success of the syndicated comic strip *Peanuts*, one day Johnny told his friends and colleagues at work that he was going home to create his own comic strip based on cavemen. And he did just that. After developing it to his satisfaction, he sent out samples to one newspaper syndicate after another. He became discouraged at the constant rejection, even from some who never really looked it over! One day, he took time off work to try and personally sell the potential strip to a few prospective syndicates. After one discouraging "no" after another, he rescued his—unopened—sample packet from one of the newspapers that had rejected it out of hand. He was so despondent that he actually pitched the large stuffed envelope in a garbage can on the street. But then he retrieved it for one more try. It "just so happened" that at one newspaper syndicate he hadn't tried, the decision-maker in the comics department was brand new at the job and was open to new ideas and new potential strips. Johnny's *B.C.* was the first thing to land on his desk, and the rest is history. That was in 1958. Today, Johnny Hart is the most widely circulated syndicated cartoonist in the world (when you add the combined circulation of his creations *B.C.* and *Wizard of Id*)!

Persistence pays off. As Zig Ziglar says, "A big shot is a little shot that kept on shooting."[6] And a key aid to persistence is deadlines. If you're thinking in terms of major life changes, give yourself a deadline; no one else will do it for you.

CREATING YOUR OWN DEADLINES

If there's something you've been putting off, why not set a date when you'll have it finished? For example, you've been putting off painting the house for months. It's long overdue. So the first step is to break the task down into little steps. Then, decide when you will accomplish each of these steps. Make the goal realistic, yet stretching.

You remember earlier, in chapter 7, when I asked you to write down a few things you want to achieve that you've been putting off? List the three most important ones again, to reinforce these goals in your mind:

_____

_____

_____

OK, now, plan *deadlines* for these three (unless they're intangible goals, like "to be more kind"):

Deadline for Goal 1 _____

Deadline for Goal 2 _____

Deadline for Goal 3 _____

Next question: Are these realistic goals? Barring some sort of disaster (like an impending hurricane or the like) or current project deadlines, what's to keep you from achieving this goal? Think right now for a moment of how good you will feel when you achieve this thing. What benefit will you draw from it?

For years and years, I put off making some scrapbooks from "souvenirs," postcards, ticket stubs (for special trips), etc. All these things were accumulating in a long box that seemed to expand over time until the items were overflowing. I finally set aside a certain Sunday that, no matter what happened, by the time I went to bed those items would have been sifted through, sorted, pasted, and taped into a scrapbook, with the garbage thrown away. I ended up taking five to six hours doing this, filling three scrapbooks. They might not be the best-organized or the best-looking, but by golly, I achieved my goal, thanks to the deadline.

CONCLUSION

Setting deadlines is helpful in order to avoid procrastination. Some deadlines are under our control. Some are not. There's one deadline that will affect us all, and yet it is not under our control. It's not pleasant to think about, but that deadline is death itself. "It is appointed unto men once to die, but after this the judgment."[7] The best one could hope for with that deadline is to be prepared at a moment's notice because "man knows not the hour" that our end will come.

There's another deadline that virtually all of us in America are affected by—the deadline of April 15. How many people would do their taxes each year if there were no due date? Or no teeth to the due date? I doubt many would, human nature being what it is. Let deadlines work for you, both those imposed from without (like the April 15 deadline the IRS forces on us) or those imposed from within (personal deadlines you project for yourself). Using deadlines is one of the most effective keys to keeping procrastination in check.

© Creators Syndicate, Inc.

Chapter 10

© Creators Syndicate, Inc.

DO THE WORST FIRST

Young people tell what they are doing,
old people what they have done,
and fools what they wish to do.
—Anonymous

I n second grade Kirsti had an old man for a substitute teacher, and one day he told this story:

> A lonely old hermit had some old porridge left over and he didn't want to waste it, so he decided to eat it. The porridge was so old and disgusting that mold had started to form around the edges of the bowl. So the old man poured himself a glass of brandy and put it beside the bowl and said to himself, "If you eat the porridge, you may have the drink." The man ate the porridge, and then he poured the drink back in the bottle and said to himself, "I sure fooled you this time."

Kirsti remarks:

> I hated that story, everything about it was wrong. First, an old man shouldn't be by himself; where was his family? Second, it's bad for you to eat old, moldy food; you can get seriously sick from it. Third, when he had finished, he should have had his reward, even though the picture of an old man drinking alone seemed awfully wrong too.

When your mom told you to eat your vegetables before the ice cream, that was not just good nutritional advice; the principle applies to life in general and can help free the procrastinator from his or her nasty habit. However, it must be administered slowly and with caution—lest the hard-core procrastinator get scared off. The purpose of this chapter is to explore the vegetables first (i.e., work before pleasure) phenomenon and also to see how rewarding yourself can help you overcome procrastination. Part of our discussion on rewards will make the case for delayed gratification.

© Creators Syndicate, Inc.

DOING THE UNPLEASANT THING FIRST

The author Edwin Bliss says in his book *Getting Things Done,* "The procrastinator thinks something like this, 'This task must be done but it is unpleasant. Therefore I will put it off as long as I can!' But the effective person thinks like this, 'This task is unpleasant, but it must be done. Therefore, I will do it now, so I can get it behind me.'"[1] Some effective people make it their goal to do at least one unpleasant task first thing in the morning, because it's a good feeling to have it over and done with.

All of us have things we enjoy doing and things we dislike in our normal work days. Let's say you like making phone calls and dislike writing reports. In that case, it's a good idea to write the report first (get it out of the way) and then enjoy making your phone calls.

I find that it's easier to go the gym in the morning and get my exercise over with then. Not that I don't enjoy it. It's just that it seems easier to get it out of the way early on. If I don't, I might not get to it.

GETTING A LITTLE PHILOSOPHICAL

One of the things that separates humans from animals is the ability to plan for the future, to think ahead, and to weigh different options. One of Socrates' students, Aristippus (c. 435–366 B.C.), claimed that the greatest good is pleasure, and the greatest evil is pain. This pleasure philosophy was developed further by Epicurus (341–270 B.C.). One of his main points was delayed gratification. Epicurus said that the result of an action must always be weighed against the possible side effects. If you have ever overeaten or binged on candy, you know what he means. He also said that short-term pleasure must be weighed against long-term pleasure. For example, a twelve-year-old boy might feel that candy is great but that a new bicycle is even better. So he saves up his money for a whole year—giving up candy—in order to have a new bike.

A family from "up north" moved to Florida and discovered a fruit tree in their backyard. After a few weeks, green citrus fruit appeared, and they said, "Great! We have limes." So they picked the "limes"—only to discover they weren't limes, and they didn't taste good. A few more weeks passed, and the "limes" turned yellow, and they said, "Great! We have lemons." So they picked the "lemons"—only to discover that they weren't lemons, and they didn't taste good. More weeks passed, and their "lemons" turned orange, and they said, "Great! We have tangerines." And this time, they were right; and this time they were delicious. The fruit that got to stay on the tree until it was ripe became what it was supposed to be all along, tangerines, but it took months. Meanwhile, the fruit that was picked prematurely was no good. Everything has its time. Only the knowledge of how good something will be *if we wait* keeps us from picking fruit too early. A lot of other things in life also need time, and we are better off if we delay gratification.

The principle of delayed gratification is essential to overcoming procrastination. While each moment that we work toward a goal might not be pleasant, we can look forward to the joy of the end result. For example, the pain of childbirth can be endured because the result—a new baby—is so glorious.

Even our Lord endured the cross for the "joy that was set before Him."[2] That joy was the salvation of all who would believe. Similarly, a lot of Christians, both today and throughout the ages, have given up earthly things for eternal ones. Jim Elliot, the martyred missionary, said, "He is no fool who gives up that which he cannot keep, to gain that which he cannot lose."[3] Is this not the ultimate delayed gratification?

Now, a discerning reader may well ask: "Wait a minute. . . . doesn't this advice of doing the unpleasant thing first contradict the earlier chapter about momentum, where you said, do what's easiest first (when choosing among equally important tasks)?" "Ah!" I hear you cry. My answer is, "Yes, it does contradict that advice!" (Go to the head of the class!) And if you had to choose between doing the unpleasant thing first or doing the easiest thing first, my advice would be to do the unpleasant thing first—*if* you're going to do it! But that's a big *if*. We've already seen that a key to overcoming procrastination is just getting started. So if there's going to be a delay here, then by all means do the easiest first. Put it this way: If it's an either/or between inactivity (not starting because you don't want to do the unpleasant task first) or activity (starting by doing the easiest task first), then by all means choose activity over inactivity—do the easiest thing first. However, if it's a situation of both/and between activity (that is unpleasant and must be done) and activity (that is easiest to do and also must be done), then choose the unpleasant task; choose to delay gratification.

THE PURITAN WORK ETHIC— DELAYED GRATIFICATION IN ACTION

© Creators Syndicate, Inc.

Do you realize that a large part of the reason the free enterprise system in the United States has been so successful is because of delayed gratification put into practice? What I'm talking about is the whole Puritan work ethic which, in its own way, represents a good form of procrastination. They delayed gratification. They put off their full enjoyment of the fruits of their labors so that they could reinvest their profits.

The interesting irony here is that the procrastinator puts off the wrong thing! He wants the fruit of his labor before he works for it! He's like the guy who goes to the fireplace and says, "I'll put firewood on, but first you give me the fire."[4] Ridiculous, you say! But so is the procrastinator's obsession with consumption now. The prosperous person, in contrast, puts off consumption and gets right to work.

It takes discipline to wait for what we want. In a society where people want what they want when they want it, it is not easy to wait for your reward. In the long run, though, anything worthwhile, anything of value, is achieved through discipline and hard work. Developing good habits of self-discipline is the ultimate antidote to overcoming procrastination.

One time one friend (let's call him Smith) rebuked another friend (let's call him Jones) for working on many Saturdays. Jones couldn't provide for his family on his normal salary, and he was definitely improving his lot in life by that extra hard work. He also made sure he spent plenty of time with his wife and children. Meanwhile, Mr. and Mrs. Smith were living the full extent of the American Dream—by running up credit card debt! At last check, Mr. Jones was on his way to building a satisfying life, and the Smiths were going through a nasty divorce. Delayed gratification is rewarding. Mr. Jones is what I call "a smart procrastinator"—he

© Creators Syndicate, Inc.

puts off consumption and gratification in order to reinvest his time, money, and effort for a future payoff. Mr. Smith, on the other hand, is just a hard-core procrastinator.

THE CARROT ON THE STICK

If you have lived a life of putting things off, you cannot expect to wake up tomorrow full of self-discipline. You must start slowly. Any achievement, large or small, requires that we give up something we want. (I want lunch; but I also want to finish this chapter, so I won't eat until I'm finished.) Just as a baby learns to walk one step at a time, so must we gradually establish new habits and ways of life. It has been said that it takes twenty-one days to establish a new habit. We develop new habits one little step at a time.

An excellent way of helping to change habits is by giving ourselves predetermined rewards—rewards unrelated to the work. This is the old "carrot on the stick" principle. If you tie a stick with a carrot dangling at the end of a string to the front of a donkey, the animal will walk in order to get the carrot, but the carrot moves with the donkey; therefore, it is always in front and it keeps him moving. Just make sure your donkey gets to eat the carrot at

rēward´ vt.
something you get -

for doing something you wouldn't ordinarily do.

if it wasn't for the reward.

© Creators Syndicate, Inc.

some point, otherwise it won't work the next time! To hold a "carrot" out that never will be enjoyed is nothing more than a broken promise, and it should never be done to ourselves nor to others. So enjoy your "carrot" when the work is done.

Rewards aren't necessary of course. Achievement is. But if rewards help you to work toward achievement, then let them work for you. It is true that "virtue is its own reward;" doing the right thing is rewarding. However, it is one thing to *know* what we should do and another thing to actually *do* it. Because of our human tendency to take the path of least resistance, we often need rewards and motivation to do what we need to do. As Lucy Hedrick, the author of *Five Days to an Organized Life*, points out: "If completing the task were reward enough, in and of itself, we would all do everything we set out to do."[5] Ergo, we need little rewards!

The treats we give ourselves can be little and simple, like a coffee break or a phone call to a friend, or large and expensive, like a vacation or buying ourselves that special something we have wanted for a long time.

By rewarding yourself at different steps along the way, your road to accomplishment will be smoother and easier. Earlier we discussed the divide and conquer principle. After dividing the procrastinated task down into bite-sized minitasks, decide how you will reward yourself after each minitask (or if the minitasks are very small, you can reward yourself after finishing a few of them). This helps to add a little incentive. If this is an important task you've been putting off, maybe you could dangle before you a major carrot for taking the first real steps toward fulfilling the goal. After all, you will have finally gotten started!

Lucy Hedrick differentiates three levels of carrots on the stick: 1) fifteen-minute rewards; 2) two-to-three hour rewards; and 3) a whole day off. It's not hard to picture what to do with two-to-three hour rewards or whole day rewards, but what about fifteen-minute ones? Hedrick lists out several different potential rewards:

- 🕐 enjoying a cup of coffee
- 🕐 skimming through a favorite section of the paper
- 🕐 walking around the block
- 🕐 stopping at a park and lying under a tree (I'd be afraid of falling asleep)
- 🕐 skipping stones on a pond
- 🕐 browsing in a favorite store[6]

Ones that I would add to that list would include reading a short passage in a book, eating a bowl of cereal or ice cream with coffee, going for a quick swim, or listening to a favorite song or piece of music. For me, a reward is often reading all six of the questions on a Trivial Pursuit card to see how many I can get right.

How about for you? Think for a minute. What things would you consider a reward for yourself? List potential items that would be a suitable reward for you. Generally, these are things that can be done in ten to fifteen minutes or less:

_____

_____

_____

_____

_____

_____

_____

_____

© Creators Syndicate, Inc.

When you make your to-do list, jot down in the margin or underneath each item one of these kinds of rewards. Then when you've completed that particular step, take a moment and give yourself that little reward. It's just a nice way to build momentum and to keep it.

Some tasks are thankless jobs. It's easy to put them off because they have little or no built-in rewards. That's why these little, unrelated rewards can be so helpful.

Sometimes a job is so big and the goal so far out of reach that we need little rewards along the way. Grades (if they're good) are temporary rewards on our way to graduation, but many a parent has built in extra rewards for good grades because the goal is far away and may seem irrelevant to the student's daily life.

Life has many pleasures. God has put good and beautiful things all around us. One caveat to consider is that we should be careful to not view every pleasure as a reward. God's gifts are neither earned nor deserved. The unexpected and the undeserved joys of life make it rich and wonderful. Rewards are just a tool to help us discipline ourselves, not a way to look at joys and pleasures.

REWARDS FOR WAKING UP IN THE MORNING

If you have trouble waking up in the morning, try and come up with a way to reward yourself for it. Years ago, when a particular cereal first came out, I enjoyed eating it so

© Creators Syndicate, Inc.

much that I put the box of cereal right by the alarm clock so that I would have an extra incentive to get up. When I first went "on-line" with the computer, I had access to the *latest breaking news* directly from the wire services, (e.g., the Associated Press). I remember bounding out of bed with the reward before me of cruising—no, crawling—around the information superhighway. It was reward enough to me to get me out of the sack. So if you struggle with rising in the morning, find some reward to help you jump-start your day.

Interestingly, the wish to sleep a little more is not a new problem. Solomon the Wise wrote, "How long will you lie there, you sluggard? When will you get up from your sleep? A little sleep, a little slumber, a little folding of the hands to rest—and poverty will come on you like a bandit and scarcity like an armed man."[7]

Does a kid *ever* have a problem getting up out of bed on Christmas morning? No way. Even if they're groggy, they bounce out of bed long before their parents do, and eagerly await the unwrapping of their gifts.

The beautifully wrapped gifts that have not been opened until Christmas Day are an example of delayed gratification in action. If a spoiled child were to tear open each gift as soon as it went under the tree (long before Christmas), then there would be nothing to look forward to. But the child is rewarded by waiting until Christmas. The child might have looked at the gifts and read the labels. She might even have shaken them, but as long as she doesn't open them, the anticipation builds. Knowing it's for her—but not yet—adds to the attraction. So the gift may get handled, squeezed, and admired. It lays there as a dream and a concrete proof of the good to come on Christmas morning. In a sense, the expectation becomes a gift in itself in that we are teaching our children a simple form of delayed gratification.

Flail:

1-23

© Creators Syndicate, Inc.

SUCCESS REINFORCES ITSELF

Reward yourself *after* completion of a task (or a minitask), not prematurely. Success itself then reinforces itself. If you get to the point where getting it done (for example, the completion of doing your taxes) feels so good that the feeling of accomplishment in itself is a reward, then great! You're well on your way to nipping procrastination in the bud.

CONCLUSION

To achieve anything, we need to put off wanting what we want when we want it. In our spoiled age, it's hard for many to learn that. Many couples starting out today attempt to gain more accoutrements of the good life than their parents ever accumulated—only the parents bought their's with cash, when they could afford to pay for it. In contrast, the young couples are buying their's on credit when they really can't afford it. And this often brings heavy debt, anxiety, arguing, bankruptcy, divorce, and misery. Where did they go wrong? They put the rewards before the work. There's a time and a place for everything. A time to work; a time to be rewarded for our work; a time to delay gratification; a time to be satisfied. So eat your vegetables—then enjoy your dessert. Such culinary advice is a good principle for all of life.

Chapter 11

© Creators Syndicate, Inc.

ESTABLISH ACCOUNTABILITY

So then each of us shall give account of himself to God.
—The Apostle Paul

H ave you ever noticed how some people are always asking you about something (let's call it Project X) that you've been putting off? You dread running into them because you know they will ask you about it. Finally, just to get them off your back, you stop procrastinating and do Project X.

© Creators Syndicate, Inc.

One of the most effective tools to keep a procrastinator from procrastinating is accountability. We've already looked in depth at one form of accountability that does wonders for the procrastinator: deadlines. Deadlines are a calendarized form of accountability; a deadline is accountability with a date attached to it.

But there are many things we tend to put off that don't necessarily have a date attached to them. Let's begin with a powerful example of how accountability helps those who have been putting off losing weight.

ACCOUNTABILITY AND WEIGHT LOSS

There are many people who struggle with excess weight. They lose pounds, then regain them. Then lose them again, then regain it all back, and so on. It's a vicious cycle. But the most effective way I have ever heard about to cut out that weight and to keep it off involves accountability in one way or another. For example, there are those who hire fitness coaches. These coaches hold their clients accountable with weigh-ins and measurements. Suddenly, goals that have been only dreamed about are being achieved because they have a coach. But most of us can't afford a fitness coach.

OK. No problem. There are other ways to be held accountable. For example, there are the various groups that meet—on a regular basis—wherein the attendees encourage one another by sharing their experiences. These include:

- ⏱ Weight Watchers
- ⏱ TOPS (Taking Off Pounds Sensibly)
- ⏱ Overeaters Anonymous

Now there are even weight-loss programs like this in the church, such as First Place. The success of these groups boils down to the accountability to which they hold their members. There are also commercial groups for weight loss that work toward the same goal. Accountability, I believe, is the single most effective way by which all these groups help their clients shed excess body baggage.

ACCOUNTABILITY GOES BEYOND HEAD KNOWLEDGE

Why does accountability work? Because it forces you to choose between the lesser of two undesirables—either doing something you'd rather do later or being embarrassed for not having done it. For many people, it is not enough just to know that you should do a certain thing, even if you're convinced you are going to do it (one of these days . . . er . . . weeks . . . er . . . months . . . er . . . years!). We sometimes need that extra little push that accountability gives us. If there's something (let's call it Project Y) that you've been meaning to do, but you keep putting it off, then consider enlisting the help of someone else. Sometimes it even helps you to mention in conversation that you plan to work on Project Y today. Just knowing that you said it and that they might later ask you about your progress on it helps you do the task. If that is not enough, then request of someone—your spouse or a reliable friend—to call you tomorrow (or next week, depending on how long it should take to complete Project Y) to ask you if you finished it. Knowing that they will call you tomorrow and ask you about this should help you get going. If you're a hard-core procrastinator, ask them to not only ask you about Project Y. Ask them to make you let them examine it for themselves!

By the way, be careful whom you choose to hold you accountable. If you get someone who's never satisfied with anything, you're setting yourself up for needless failure.

THE IMPORTANCE OF THE QUALITY OF OUR WORK

One aspect about accountability merits warning. We need to be careful because we can sometimes fool others about the quality of our work. But in the long run, if we cheat others, we're cheating ourselves.

It's one thing to not procrastinate. It's another thing to do things in a rather shoddy way. In college, there was an expression about how students should write or speak when being evaluated by their professors: "If you can't dazzle them with your brilliance, baffle them with your baloney."

Have you ever heard of a "Potemkin Village"? Its origin goes back to the time when Grigori Potemkin supposedly pulled a fast one on Catherine the Great. It seems this guy was a classic procrastinator and in some ways a classic example of a fraud. He was probably the most notable administrator for Catherine the Great, who ruled Russia in the last part of the eighteenth century. Having no religious scruples, Catherine had a series of lovers, of which Potemkin was probably the longest-lasting. Potemkin was responsible for adding a lot of southern territory to Russia during those years, including the Crimea. In early 1787, the Czarina wanted to visit all these great new places, for which she had been sending Potemkin funds. She not only wanted to see them for herself, but she wanted to show these new villages off to diplomats from all over Europe who joined her on a long sleigh ride for that purpose. Although she had sent him many resources for the building up of the interior, Potemkin had apparently squandered some of them on "mistresses, liquor, and food." And now the Czarina herself was coming to view the great additions to her empire! Accountability. As her convoy of 170 or so sleighs trudged south in the bitter cold, Potemkin went ahead of them to make things appear better than they actually were. Here's what historians Will and Ariel Durant write of the incident:

> Every town on the route, warned and instructed by Potemkin, was on its best behavior, washed and dressed as never before, happy for a day. . . . Along the [Dnieper] river Catherine saw the "Potemkin villages" which [he] had primed and polished for her pleasure, and perhaps to impress the diplomats with the prosperity of Russia. Some of the prosperity had been improvised by Potemkin, some of it was real. "That he created sham villages along the banks, and marshaled the peasantry to create the illusion of progress was the fantastic invention of a Saxon diplomatist." Catherine herself was probably not deceived, but she may have concluded . . . that even if half the prosperity and neatness of those towns was a passing show, the actuality of [the region]—town, forts, and port, built on Crimean shores in two years—was enough to merit Potemkin praise.[1]

© Creators Syndicate, Inc.

Today, two hundred years later, "a Potemkin village" refers to a sham. The point is, be ready at a moment's notice. Have your work ready to be inspected. Potemkin made it just in time, but what if he had somehow hit a snag in his trip just ahead of her?

In the New Testament, we are told of the day of accountability when our works will be tested, as it were, by fire. Paul writes in his epistle to the church at Corinth:

> If any man builds on this foundation [of Jesus Christ] using gold, silver, costly stones, wood, hay or straw, his work will be shown for what it is, because the Day will bring it to light. It will be revealed with fire, and the fire will test the quality of each man's work. If what he has built survives, he will receive his reward. If it is burned up, he will suffer loss; he himself will be saved, but only as one escaping through the flames.[2]

Thus, there is no value in being accountable to others on a superficial basis. In the long run, the real substance of our work will be tested—if not here on earth, than surely on Judgment Day. This leads me to my next point—accountability before God.

ACCOUNTABILITY BEFORE HIM WHO IS OMNISCIENT AND OMNIPRESENT

For some people the greatest help in overcoming procrastination is the knowledge that we have a Father in heaven who is always observing us. We are always under His watchful eye, and one day we will give an account to Him for what we've done with our time and all the other resources He has given us. This accountability can make people conscientious even for minor things. For example, here's a conversation that actually took place one day between my wife and our daughter:

"Mom, why do you clean *under* the rug?" asked Annie.

"I clean under the rug because it's dirty," answered Mom.

"But nobody can see under the rug, Mom."

"God can see under rugs, and He knows if it's clean or not, and that's reason enough to clean under the rugs. We want to take good care of the house He has lent us, so we keep it clean."

Although there was no inspector coming to check under the rug, there is Someone who sees and knows. Whether you agree or not with this particular example, the point is well-taken. Substantive work will last—just like the medieval Cathedrals that have lasted through the centuries, survived two world wars, and still amaze visitors today. They were built not only to house the parish; they were built for the glory of God.

This accountability to God can keep us in line perhaps more than anything else, and it is also the basis for the Christian work ethic. All work is done to please our Father in heaven, and all of our lives are an open book before Him.

© Creators Syndicate, Inc.

People often do their work only to be seen by others. They might not work hard if the boss is away (if there's not a means for accountability built in). But this is not the way it should be. When people only do their work well if they are watched and closely supervised, and slack off every time they believe themselves to be alone, then productivity goes down. It doesn't always matter that everybody sees your most excellent work; you know it's excellent, and, more importantly, God knows you did well.

Ronald Reagan had a plaque on his desk (right next to the jelly beans) reading something like this:

> It's amazing how much work can be done,
> if we don't care who gets the credit.

Now, I'm a firm believer in giving credit where credit is due, but in one sense, credit is not the be-all end-all. Why? Because God knows, that's why. He knows if I did a good job or not. He knows how hard I worked on a project someone else might have received the credit for. God knows, and He is just. His justice ensures fair payment for me, whether it's in this world or in the next. (We're back to delayed gratification!)

Some people might think that working for a heavenly reward is just "pie in the sky" when you die by and by, but Jesus Himself said that we should do our work for God in a quiet and discrete way so that our "Father who sees in secret will Himself reward you openly."[3] I'm sure there will be many upsets on the Day of Accountability. Some people well-known and well-loved in this life will be exposed for the frauds they are. Meanwhile, little old "nobodies" in this world will shine like stars in the firmament. I know I'm getting a little heavy for a book of this nature, but if such sublime and sobering thoughts don't motivate the hard-core procrastinator, nothing else will!

PARABLE OF THE TALENTS

Consider the classic parable you've probably heard many times, the parable of the talents. Do you realize it has something powerful to say about procrastination? Jesus told a story about three men who were entrusted by their master with talents (a form of money). The master then went away on a trip. When he returned, he learned that two of the men were faithful and diligent servants who used the talents to gain more. But the third guy buried his talent, and for this he was severely lambasted. "You should have at least put it in the bank where it would have earned interest!" he was told.[4] And so it is with many who procrastinate. We bury our God-given talents. And the world is poorer for it—and we are poorer for it. An interesting detail in this story is that when the first servant received his talents, he *immediately* went to work on it. *Immediately.*

CONCLUSION

If you find yourself hopelessly procrastinating, employ the buddy system. Find someone who will help you by making you answer to them about those things you are putting off. As we've seen, accountability can help put the habit of procrastination in check. But perhaps even more effective is accountability before God. Let me tell you about my mother-in-law. (She's so nice that it's hard to tell mother-in-law jokes!) One time she was working as a telephone operator in her country (which is Norway), and the management had developed a new method of supervision. At any time they could listen in on any conversation between the operators and the clients. This caused a lot of protest from the operators, but she did not mind at all. Why? "Because," she said, "I am supervised from a much higher authority than the management of the telephone company. I will one day answer to God Himself. He knows everything I say and do, and I am accountable to Him." Hmmmmm. You see? Some mother-in-law. Thus we see, whether before God or man, accountability can be a powerful way to nip procrastination in the bud!

© Creators Syndicate, Inc.

Chapter 12

© Creators Syndicate, Inc.

FINAL CONSIDERATIONS: BALANCING LIFE'S COMPETING DEMANDS

So teach us to number our days,
That we may gain a heart of wisdom.
—Psalm 90:12, NKJV

One of my favorite comedians, Stan Laurel, once said, "Life isn't short enough" in a context where it was obvious he meant to say, "Life is too short." Isn't it though? Therefore, we want to make the best of our time.

In this chapter, we want to mull over some final considerations—including the urgent vs. the important; building in "margin" to our lives; the problem of entropy; and balancing life's competing demands. We conclude with a quick review of our six steps for overcoming procrastination.

SOME THINGS BETTER LEFT UNDONE

I am not a member of the Procrastinators Club of America (I never got around to sending in my application!). But I think they have a point when they say that there are some things that should be procrastinated . . . indefinitely. In other words, some things we put off are best left undone—forever! Les Waas, one time president of the Procrastinators Club of America, once said: "We feel that the ultimate thing to procrastinate against is war. Just think, if you keep putting off wars, eventually you might forget what you wanted to fight about."[1] While this is a clever point, it obviously reflects a faulty view of human nature. While the good guys put off such things, the bad guys would have no such scruples! The nations of Europe would have been in much better shape (circa 1940) had they been better prepared for the monster that was Hitler. He laid out his strategy for all the world to see in *Mein Kampf* (published in 1925). But, the Procrastinators Club is absolutely right that some things *are* best left undone. Or they're best left undone by us.

Some people feel a sense of false guilt because they think they have to do more than they could possibly do! In other words, they have a messiah complex. They couldn't possibly do all the things

© Creators Syndicate, Inc.   12·30

that they think in the back of their heads they should be doing. So they feel guilty because they're not doing them. This is why it's so helpful to take the obituary test (as we discussed in chapter 6) to figure out what your priorities and goals are and then plan accordingly. For any reader dealing with such a false guilt, I repeat: some things are best left undone— at least by *you*. This shows, then, the need to carefully differentiate between what is truly important and what is urgent.

THE URGENT VS. THE IMPORTANT

Sometimes we don't attend to important things we should do only because the urgent things crowd out the important things. Thus, we must decide what is urgent versus what is important. Charles Hummel in *Tyranny of the Urgent* writes:

> We live in constant tension between the urgent and the important. The problem is that the important task rarely must be done today, or even this week. Extra hours of prayer and Bible study, a visit with that non-Christian friend, careful study of an important book: these projects can wait. But the urgent tasks call for instant action—endless demands pressure every hour and day. . . . The momentary appeal of [urgent] tasks seems irresistible and important, and they devour our energy. But in the light of time's perspective their deceptive prominence fades; with a sense of loss we recall the important tasks pushed aside. We realize we've become slaves to the tyranny of the urgent.[2]

Hummel makes the point that we should be careful to not let the daily *urgent* tasks bog us down to the point where we overlook what we really should be doing (the *important* tasks). Of course, if you can't see your desk for the paperwork or you can't see the kitchen counter for the dirty dishes, you might have some cleaning up to do before you can go on. Putting off cleaning up or getting organized tends to make what should be a manageable task enormous and overwhelming.

Taking breaks (short ones, long ones) is often helpful because they allow us to refocus on what's truly important versus what's urgent (but not necessarily important). Some of the urgent activities that vie for our attention may be in that category we spoke of earlier: things better left undone, at least by us.

I can't stand the many telemarketing phone calls we Americans receive nowadays. It seems they have some sort of signal at their end to make sure they call you just when you sit down to eat! Or worse, when you take a bath. Answering that phone call is an urgent item, not necessarily an important one. Florida (and I imagine this is true for other states as well) has a service whereby,

for a modest fee, state officials put your name on a list of households that should not receive any calls from *legitimate* telemarketers. We subscribe to that service, and it has been great! The urgency of receiving many phone calls (that aren't important) has been eliminated. Now, all we get are the important calls—like the ones to our teenage daughter from all her friends!

Differentiating between the urgent and the important and eliminating the "non-important, urgent" items eliminates needless stress

© Creators Syndicate, Inc.

and clutter in our lives. Another thing that avoids needless stress involves building in "margin" to our lives.

AVOID "MARGINLESS" LIVING

Richard Swenson, M.D., author of *Margin: Restoring Emotional, Physical, Financial, and Time Reserves to Overloaded Lives,* advocates that we build in protection, buffer zones—what he calls "margins"—to our busy lives. These margins essentially state: "thus far and no more." Dr. Swenson writes:

> The conditions of modern-day living devour margin. . . . Margin . . . is having breath left at the top of the staircase, money left at the end of the month, and sanity left at the end of adolescence. . . .
>
> Marginless is fatigue; margin is energy.
> Marginless is red ink; margin is black ink.
> Marginless is hurry; margin is calm.
> Marginless is anxiety; margin is security.
> Marginless is reality; margin is remedy.
> Marginless is the disease of the 1990s.
> Margin is the cure.[3]

Dr. Swenson points out that *good relationships* are what's needed to build in "margin" to our lives. Unfortunately, the hectic pace of modern life devours these relationships, the very safeguards that protect us from the harm of modern stress! Thus, it becomes a vicious cycle. Tragically, there's a high price we're paying for the breakdown of the family. Dr. Swenson writes:

© Creators Syndicate, Inc.

Nearly all indices of the scripturally prescribed relational life have suf-
fered major setbacks over the last three decades. Marriage—worse; par-
enting—worse; the extended family—worse; the sense of community—
worse; social-support systems—worse; church commitment—worse;
church unity—worse; and one-anothering in the church—worse. And it
happened seemingly overnight. Little wonder our pains are so acute.[4]

We suffer from a great deal of overload in this country. Swenson catalogues the following things with which we are often overburdened:

- Activity overload
- Change overload
- Choice overload
- Commitment overload
- Competition overload
- Debt overload
- Decision overload
- Education overload
- Expectation overload

- 🕓 Fatigue overload
- 🕓 Hurry overload
- 🕓 Information overload
- 🕓 Media overload
- 🕓 Ministry overload
- 🕓 Noise overload
- 🕓 People overload
- 🕓 Pollution overload
- 🕓 Possession overload
- 🕓 Problem overload
- 🕓 Technology overload
- 🕓 Traffic overload
- 🕓 Waste overload
- 🕓 Work overload[5]

He adds, ". . . chronic overloading is not God's will. It is okay to draw a line."[6]

TIME OUT

We have been given a margin every week by God, and that is the Sabbath. God knew we needed a day of rest, and He instituted it at the time of creation. If we allow ourselves to work just as usual on Sundays, we will soon find out that our mind and bodies will pay the price of overload. If your job forces you to have to work on Sunday, then consider changing positions or at least choose another day to take time off. Also, seek out some other way to spend time with God (e.g., Sunday evening service or a Bible study during the week) if you're forced to work during church time.

Planning ahead is also a form of time-out. I find it helpful to spend some time "evaluating." I take a fresh legal pad, sit down quietly, and then just let ideas come and write them out. This time might seem wasteful at first glance, because it may seem like just sitting and doing nothing. But in the long run, these quiet moments when we just let our thoughts flow can often yield great ideas. For example, years ago I did not have a study at home. In thinking through this problem, I came up with a solution. In the living room, where I had four tall bookshelves, I arranged them in an L-shape (facing away from the corner), and I put my desk in the corner. This way I had a little cubby hole for an office. It worked well until we were eventually able to move into a new house that had a separate room for a study. Even dreams are good to put down on paper, for nothing becomes a plan or a goal that wasn't an idea first.

When you evaluate problems like this, jotting down all sorts of ideas (many of which may be off the wall, but that's OK too), it is like digging for treasures. You might find something of great value. I try to take time out for this at least a few times a week.

© Creators Syndicate, Inc.

Vacations are also necessary time-outs. They help us gain a fresh perspective, as we get away and recharge our batteries. Sometimes we need our minds cleared and our thoughts refocused. This is hard to do at home when the phone rings, and the laundry needs doing, and thousands of tasks demand our attention. When we go away and have a change of scenery—someplace where we can't be reached by our everyday tasks—then we have a chance to regroup, refocus, and regain our strength and our vision for the work we need to do. Although presidents (of the United States) are extremely busy, it sometimes seems they're always on vacation or on the golf course! But how can they be effective if they don't take many breaks?

Years ago, I took a summer sabbatical from work. We were considering becoming full-time missionaries, but we wanted to do it on an internship basis first. Thankfully, we received the opportunity to do just that. While we were away from our home and the jobs and the house (and even the country), an important long-range goal began to finally take shape: the desire to write a book. We were able to write up a detailed proposal for the idea, and when we got back into the country, I was able to convert the proposal into reality (in large part thanks to Dr. D. James Kennedy, with whom I co-wrote the book). That book was the best-selling (more than 100,000 copies in print) *What If Jesus Had Never Been Born?* Had my family and I not gotten away from our normal routine, with all the hustle and bustle, I wonder if the book would ever have come about! It's important to get away, to take vacations or breaks. It helps us to better manage ourselves, and when we're managing ourselves well, generally procrastination is in check.

RECOGNIZING THE INEVITABILITY OF ENTROPY

One of the reasons it's so hard to overcome procrastination is entropy. If you remember from your basic physics lessons, the Second Law of Thermodynamics (entropy) means this:

- Everything breaks down.
- Everything goes from order to chaos.
- Everything goes from working to malfunctioning.
- Everything goes from being fixed to being broken.
- Everything goes from being new to being old.

This principle of entropy makes it hard to keep up with everything. Nothing (material) lasts forever. Even some of the best-made stuff must sooner or later return to dust. The forces of decay are always at work; we were always fighting entropy. It is often the unexpected event that messes up our well-laid plans and throws off a tight schedule. The car breaks down, and we have to spend time getting it to the mechanic and waiting for it to be fixed. Unanticipated expenses throw off the budget as well. The fence (or portions of it) falls over during a storm. The washing machine quits, and the air conditioner doesn't seem to work right. Your clothes get worn out, and the food we had saved for later is only fit to be thrown out. No wonder procrastination comes so easily! You don't have to do anything to procrastinate.

In the margins of our lives, we need to build in room for entropy. When it takes us by surprise, we need to deal with it as a part of life, even though it can be a nuisance. For example, an effective financial budget calls for setting aside money for car maintenance, so when the car needs to go in for repair, the money's already there. Thus, part of keeping on top of procrastination involves recognizing the inevitable fact of entropy and planning ahead.

THE BALANCING ACT

Life has been accurately described as a balancing act between competing demands. There are many competing voices for our time and our attention. A successful life achieves

© Creators Syndicate, Inc.

the best balance between these competing demands. Procrastination spoils a healthy balance, and the juggling balls come crashing down.

REVIEW OF SIX WAYS TO HELP KEEP PROCRASTINATION IN CHECK

As we close out the book, let's quickly recall all the steps we discussed earlier, the six techniques I've suggested to help overcome the habit of procrastination.

1) Determine your priorities. Decide if certain tasks are necessary in the first place. If they are, then the next five steps apply to these particular tasks.
2) Break down those tasks you are putting off into many minitasks. Making such a list is the first of these minitasks. When a task is broken down into manageable steps, it no longer looks so foreboding.
3) Prioritize those minitasks. If all steps are equally important to take, then do the easiest first so that you build momentum.

4) Give yourself a realistic, but challenging, deadline if there isn't one already attached to this project.

5) Reward yourself at various stages along the way, especially in the early stages when you need to begin.

6) If all else fails, enlist the help of buddies to hold you accountable.

Put these steps to work for you, and soon you too will be a recovering procrastinator!

© Creators Syndicate, Inc.

EACH DAY "A NEW YEAR"

I once interviewed a motivational speaker, "America's Attitude Coach," Ray Peletier, who lost more than a hundred pounds in a couple of years. He got tired of having to ask the stewardesses for the extra clip-on clip for the seat belt on the many airline flights he took. When he finally decided to lose weight, he said the only way he could do it was one day at a time. He says that each day to him is January 1. This day, whatever the calendar says, is his January 1! Can you lose weight on January 1? Sure! (Unless you count those

© Creators Syndicate, Inc.

chips and nuts they serve you in the lingering moments of that New Year's Eve Party.) I think that's a great way to think of it—each day is a new beginning. This day is January 1. I think that's worth applying to the ongoing challenge of losing weight or whatever habits we struggle to change. You can't do it all at once, but you can do it one day at a time.

CONCLUSION

In the long run, the procrastinator should strive to change his habits so that the "do it now" mode is on autopilot—so that procrastination doesn't come naturally anymore. In short, we must change the *habit* of procrastination. The beauty of overcoming this habit is that you no longer have to be burdened with a lot of things you "should" have done or that you "should" be doing—realizing that there are some things we *don't* need to do. There is an enormous freedom in knowing what you want to do and then just doing it. And when we get into the habit of living this way, we keep the silent thief of procrastination at bay virtually all the time.

Soli Deo Gloria.

Epilogue

© Creators Syndicate, Inc.

SOMETHING *REALLY* IMPORTANT TO NOT PUT OFF

Procrastination is my sin.
It brings me naught but sorrow.
I know that I should stop it.
In fact, I will—tomorrow!
—Gloria Pitzer

Have you ever had a nagging suspicion that something should be done about life after death? If there is life after this existence—should it not then be planned for? As a Christian I firmly believe the Bible to be both reliable and accurate, and based on what it says, I believe eternal life to be a certainty. God says (through St. John): "I write these things to you who believe in Jesus that you may *know that you have eternal life.* . . . (emphasis added)."[1]

If you are among the procrastinators of this world, you might think that all concern for eternity can wait, that there is plenty of time to think about God later. As the years go by, we often tend to become less sensitive to the things of God, too busy with life, too comfortable, too hardened by life's knocks and bumps. So we put off making our peace with God. Around 1000 B.C. King Solomon the Wise said, "Remember your Creator in the days of your youth, before the days of trouble come and the years approach when you will say, 'I find no pleasure in them.'"2

Did you ever hear the story about the minister's dream? He was going to preach on the Bible text that says, "Now is the accepted time; behold, now is the day of salvation."3 He dreamed that he went down to the depths of hell, where he heard some devils debating as to how best to obscure the gospel message so that they could drag more people down to hell. One of them said, "Let me go. I'll tell them the Bible is just a fable. It's not the Word of God." Another one piped up and said, "No, send me. I'll tell them there is no God, no Savior, no heaven, no hell." But an older and wiser devil said, "No, they won't believe that. Send me. I'll tell them there is a God, a Savior, a heaven and hell, but I'll also tell them there is no hurry. Tomorrow will do." And all the demons agreed to send this one.

PEACE WITH GOD

Years ago I made a wonderful discovery—something that I think is not worth putting off. Peace with God. Many times the reason people put God off is because we think that He is some kind of cosmic killjoy, who will send us to some nasty place as missionaries and take away our desserts forever. God loves us! He wants the best for us. He has created us for joy and has made us for eternal life with Him.

Let me say at the outset that I'm not better than others. But I feel like I'm a beggar telling other beggars where they can find a constant source of good food! When I made my peace with God, or became a Christian, He began to transform me into what He wanted me to be. I'm far from what I should be, but thank God, I'm better than I was. And just

© Creators Syndicate, Inc.

as we like to tell others about good things we come across, so I want to tell you about the wonderful news I found years ago.

Here's the essence of what I learned: God loves us and has a purpose for our lives. But our sins put up a blockade between us and Him. Around 750 years before Christ, the Hebrew prophet Isaiah said this about that subject: "Surely the arm of the LORD is not too short to save, nor his ear too dull to hear. But your iniquities [sins] have separated you from your God; your sins have hidden his face from you, so that he will not hear."[4] In other words, God is so holy or perfect that our sins keep us from directly approaching Him. For hundreds of years, the Jews (whose religion is the base of Christianity, for which every Christian should be eternally grateful) had a very special place in the temple called the Holy of Holies, which was separated from the people by a large curtain. Only the High Priest could enter that place, and only once a year at that! When he would go into that chamber, he was in the very presence of God, who is awesome (not in the trivialized sense of the word). We can't even look at the sun directly without going blind, and that's only a thing created by God! How much less can we look directly in the face of God and live. Because it was such an awe-inspiring thing to enter into God's presence, the priest would have a few bells attached to his leg so they could hear if he was still walking around and still alive in there! Furthermore, they would tie a rope to the man to make sure that if he were to die in there—because the presence of God is so holy—his body could be pulled away, without entering that inner sanctuary. (That would not have been a fun job!) This gives us a glimpse of how awesome God really is. "It is a dreadful thing to fall into the hands of the living God."[5]

People today are often clueless about the holiness of God. In our culture, God's name is taken in vain as if it means nothing. It's interesting that even in other cultures when they swear, they don't say "Oh Buddha!" or "Oh Mohammed!" But they do say "Oh God" or "Jesus Christ!" I think everyone knows deep down who is who and Who is Who.

God hasn't changed from the time He revealed Himself in the Bible. He's still holy. There is still a gap between God, who is by nature Holy, and us, who are by nature unholy.

Jesus Christ was the only perfect person who ever lived. He was the Lamb of God, which is a reference to the Passover lamb. You will recall that the ancient Hebrews had to take an unblemished lamb, sacrifice it, and put the blood of the lamb on the top and sides of the outside of the doors so that the angel of death would pass over their homes. Christ, our Passover Lamb, was slain for us. In fact, all of the sacrifices of the Old Testament were foreshadows of Christ's death once-and-for-all. Jesus was the culmination of the sacrificial system. The Bible says, "without the shedding of blood there is no forgiveness."[6] It is the shedding of Christ's blood that brings forgiveness from God.

When Jesus died, an amazing event took place. The curtain in the temple that separated the Holy of Holies from everything else tore down the middle! This was obviously a miracle, not done by human hands. What's the point? Christ's death accomplished a great thing! Thanks to what He did for us, we have ready access to God and forgiveness from Him. Not because we're good, but because Jesus paid the price necessary for us to have peace with a holy God. ⟶ next

We need, though, to not trust in our own good works to get us to heaven—because they won't. They're not good enough. It's sort of like this. Suppose some sewage seeped into a large vat of milk in a dairy. Then suppose many cartons of milk were processed before this disaster was known. Some cartons may contain a large percentage of sewage. Some may contain very little. But they're all contaminated nonetheless. The cartons teeming with sewage would be like the mass-murderer or Hitler or Stalin. The cartons with microscopic levels of sewage would be like Mother Teresa or Billy Graham. But there's still sewage there. In their natural state, it would be unacceptable. In other words:

the PROMISE   by Wiley

THE "Seed of the woman" WOULD COME ONE DAY

TO REMOVE THEIR SINS AND TO OPEN 'THE WAY.'

A PROPHET OF OLD HAD EVEN TOLD OF THE VERY DAY THAT HE WOULD COME

AND MANY TURNED OUT TO PRAISE AND SHOUT! THO' AMONG THEM— THERE WERE SOME

WHO EXPECTED A SAVIOR, WIELDING A SWORD,

IN PLACE OF A LOVING, COMPASSIONATE LORD.

BUT HE DIDN'T COME TO SAVE THEIR DAY, NOR THE HEAD OF ROME TO SEVER,

HE CAME TO DIE— TO BECOME "THE WAY," THE WAY TO LIVE —FOREVER.

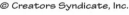

© Creators Syndicate, Inc.

"For all have sinned and fall short of the glory of God."[7] No one can make it to heaven apart from Christ's shed blood on the cross.

D. James Kennedy points out that there are really only two religions in the world—the religion of trusting in self for salvation or the religion of trusting in Christ alone and His shed blood on the cross for salvation. Trusting in self would include those of other religions who think their good works will get them to heaven. The "trusting in self" category even includes those church-goers who have never really accepted Jesus Christ as their Savior and Lord. They think they will go to heaven by their own good works. But they don't realize that even our good works are stained by our sin. We can't save ourselves; only someone bigger than us can save us. Jesus Christ is that someone. He offers us the free gift of eternal life.

Eternal life can be found right here and now. It is not something that starts after death, it starts with a new birth. When we admit that we have broken God's law (the Ten Commandments) and that we are guilty before Him, then we have taken the first step. When we turn away from our sins and accept the death of Jesus Christ as atonement, then something wonderful happens. Eternal life! It starts as soon as we truly surrender our lives to God. Gradually, throughout our lives, God makes the new life grow and flourish in us, and He slowly puts to death our sinful nature. Joy, peace, and love start to show themselves in our hearts. The day we die and reach heaven we will be totally renewed and remade, fit for heaven and perfect.

If this is what you want, you can pray this prayer, adding you own thoughts and feelings:

> Dear God, I know that I have fallen short. I have sinned against You in word, thought, and deed. I'm sorry for all my sin. And I thank You that You are merciful, and that You forgive sin based on Christ's death on the cross in our place. I accept You, Lord Jesus as my Savior and Lord,

thanking You for the salvation You provide as a free gift. Please forgive me, take my life, and make something beautiful out of it, let it count for You. Make me Your child, and make me new. Let Your eternal life start in me today and keep me safe until I see You face-to-face in heaven. In Jesus' name. Amen.

If you prayed this prayer from your heart to God, He heard you and you are now a Christian and at peace with God. Tell somebody right away. If you have wronged someone, make it right, and forgive those who have wronged you. It is important that you start reading the Bible (the Gospel of John is a good place to start) and that you talk to God in prayer. It is also important that you find a good church to belong to. If you want a free book that will help you get started, write to D. James Kennedy at Coral Ridge Ministries and ask for *Beginning Again*.[8]

If you put off saying the prayer, please consider that salvation is one thing you don't want to put off. If you don't agree or you have questions, then please feel free to look into the matter. But, for your sake, don't put this off.

God bless you.

ENDNOTES

© Creators Syndicate, Inc.

CHAPTER 1

1.   Lee Buck with Dick Schneider, *Tapping Your Secret Source of Power* (Old Tappan, NJ: Fleming H. Revell, 1985), 196.

2.   Ibid.

3.   Brian Tracy, *The Psychology of Achievement,* tape series (Chicago: Nightingale-Conant, 1984).

CHAPTER 2

1.   Zig Ziglar, *See You at the Top* (Gretna, LA: Pelican Publishing Company, 1977), 16.

2.   Ibid.

3.   Herbert V. Prochnow and Herbert V. Prochnow, Jr., *The Toastmaster's Treasure Chest* (New York: Harper & Row, Publishers, Inc., 1979), 353–354.

4.   Molly Ivins, (Los Angeles: Creators Syndicate), December 1994.

5.   *The World Almanac 1998* (Mahwah, NJ: K-III Reference Corporation, 1998), 109.

6.   TV interview with Larry Burkett, Coral Ridge Ministries, 1986.

7.   John McClain, "Baby Boomers are Putting Off Saving," Associated Press, 8 December 1997.

8.   I remember in 1981, I had my wife photograph me with my shirt off. I was showing off my "spare tire" in the "before" picture. Alas, I haven't gotten ready yet for the "after" picture. But I will . . . someday. In fact, by the time this book goes to press, I'll be down to a comfortable weight (hopefully!). Actually, I haven't been overweight all these years. It's been like a sine wave. I lose the weight and keep it off for a year or so. Then I slowly gain it back for another year. Then I lose it again, etc. Meanwhile, I've been pretty good about maintaining a physical fitness program all these years. I'm better off than my brother was when he once told me, "Oh, I'm in shape—in the shape of a pear!"

9. Some have kidded me that I should wheel around an IV with caffeine. (You know why I'm addicted? When Mom was pregnant with me, she drank a pot of coffee everyday . . . so here I am, some forty years later. I've got my excuse, what's yours? Just kidding . . . and besides, I don't drink *that* much.) So, I know how hard it is to deprive the body of that to which it is addicted. However, I also know there are tons of people who have quit smoking for good.

10. Tom Heymann, *The Unofficial U.S. Census: What the U.S. Census Doesn't Tell You* (New York: Fawcett Columbine, 1991), 40.

11. The American Cancer Society and the U.S. Center for Disease Control and Prevention report that significant changes occur if we stop lighting up. In fact, some of the changes take place literally within *minutes* of not smoking! If you quit smoking for twenty minutes, your blood pressure and your pulse return to normal. Twenty minutes! If you stop for a day (twenty-four hours), your chance of a heart attack decreases! If you quit for two days (forty-eight hours), your nerve endings start to grow again and your ability to smell and taste are improved. If you quit for a whole year, you're 50 percent less likely than a smoker to suffer from "coronary heart disease." If you stop for fifteen years, your body repairs itself as if you had never smoked at all. ("Some Benefits of Quitting Smoking," *The World Almanac 1995* [Mahwah, NJ: Funk and Wagnalls, 1994], 705. Source: American Cancer Society; U.S. Center for Disease Control and Prevention.) They also report many other benefits from not lighting up, which kick in from one to nine months later: "Coughing, sinus congestion, fatigue, shortness of breath decrease." In short, there are many benefits to not smoking.

12. Larry Davis, pilot of Delta flight 1141, *Miami Herald*, 20 August 1988.

13. Quoted in Walter B. Knight, *Knight's Master Book of New Illustrations* (Grand Rapids: Eerdmans, 1956), 520.

CHAPTER 3

1. Matthew 6:34.

2. D. James Kennedy with Jerry Newcombe, *New Every Morning* (Eugene, OR: Multnomah, 1996), entry for October 9.

3. Psalm 118:24, TLB.

4. Prochnow and Prochnow, Jr., *The Toastmaster's Treasure Chest*, 294.

5. Ibid., 343.

6. Dr. Donald E. Wildmon, "It Is Time to End the Religious Bigotry," *AFA Journal*, July 1995, 21.

7. Robert T. Michael, John H. Gagnon, Edward O. Laumann, and Gina Kolata, *Sex in America: A Definitive Survey* (Boston: Little, Brown and Company, 1994), 112, 119, 124–125.

CHAPTER 4

1. This is a paraphrase of Proverbs 26:13.
2. Proverbs 26:14.
3. Proverbs 20:13.
4. Proverbs 6:6–8.
5. Proverbs 10:26.
6. Proverbs 18:9.
7. Ecclesiastes 11:4.
8. Proverbs 20:4.
9. Ecclesiastes 11:6.
10. Ecclesiastes 10:18.
11. Denis Waitley, *The 10 Seeds of Greatness: The Ten Best Kept Secrets of Total Greatness* (Old Tappan, NJ: Fleming H. Revell, 1983), 72.
12. Lee Buck, *Tapping Your Secret Source of Power,* 197 [emphasis mine].
13. Stephen Covey, *The 7 Habits of Highly Effective People* (New York: Simon & Schuster, 1989), 71–72.
14. Zig Ziglar, *See You at the Top*, 209.
15. Zig Ziglar, *See You at the Top*, 3.
16. Ibid., 204–205.
17. James 1:5.
18. James 4:13–16.
19. Walter B. Knight, *Knight's Treasury of Illustrations* (Grand Rapids, MI: Eerdmans, 1963), 300.

CHAPTER 5

1. *Reader's Digest*, December 1982.
2. Ibid.
3. Lewis and Faye Copeland, ed., *10,000 Jokes, Toasts & Stories* (Garden City, NY: Doubleday & Company, Inc., 1965), 81.
4. Richard Swenson, M.D., *Margin: Restoring Emotional, Physical, Financial, and Time Reserves to Overloaded Lives* (Colorado Springs: NavPress, 1992), 161.

CHAPTER 6

1.   Retold by Helen Reynolds and Mary E. Tramel, *Executive Time Management: Getting 12 Hours' Work Out of an 8-Hour Day* (Englewood Cliffs, NJ: Prentice-Hall, Inc., 1979), 17–18.

2.   The Deluxe Corporation's mission statement, quoted by Jeffrey Abraham, *The Mission Statement Book* (Berkeley, CA: Ten Speed Press, 1995), 212.

3.   Delta Airline's vision statement, quoted in ibid., 211.

4.   Luke 10:38–41.

5.   Matthew 6:33, NKJV.

6.   James Dobson and Gary Bauer, *Children at Risk* (Dallas: Word Books, 1990), 157.

7.   Ibid.

CHAPTER 7

1.   Quoted in Victor M. Parachin, "Don't Put It Off! Beating the Battle with Procrastination," *The Toastmaster* 64, no. 1 (January 1998): 25.

2.   For this illustration, I'm indebted to Edwin Bliss, *Getting Things Done* (New York et al: Bantam Books, 1984).

CHAPTER 8

1.   With perfect 20/20 hindsight, many sit in judgment today on Thomas Jonathan (Stonewell) Jackson because he served the South. He was not pro-slavery. He was a devout man, of impeccable character. Long before the war, he taught blacks how to read and write using the Bible. During the war, he even donated some personal money to many of his former students, as they would be in great need of provision in war time. If Jackson had been born a few hundred miles north, in Ohio, instead of what is today West Virginia, he likely would have served the North. Be that as it may, he remains a brilliant strategist and is recognized as such by military historians.

2.   Stonewall Jackson, quoted in Ken Burn's *The Civil War*, PBS, 1989, tape 2.

3.   Paul Lee Tan, *Encyclopedia of 7700 Illustrations*, (Rockville, MD; Assurance Publishers, 1984), 1092.

4.   Buck, *Tapping Your Secret Source of Power*, 202.

5.   Elisabeth Elliot, *A Slow and Certain Light* (Waco, TX: Word, 1973), 50.

CHAPTER 9

1. *Bits & Pieces*, vol. I, no. 7, 17–18.
2. Bliss, *Getting Things Done,* 122.
3. Tony Horwitz, *Confederate in the Attic's Dispatches* (New York: Pantheon Books, 1998), 321.
4. For example, suppose you took a job at minimum wage. As of this writing, minimum wage is roughly $5 per hour. After a forty-hour work week, at $5 an hour, you would have earned before taxes in one year, only $10,400. If this is your current salary, please don't think I'm knocking you. I'm just trying to make the point you can do better, much better. There are many opportunities to learn and to improve your lot. Meanwhile, you could work full-time at a minimum-wage job and even take a second minimum-wage job, and yet that still only gives you a limited amount per year. Let's say you're able to work for an additional twenty hours per week. That means you bring in an additional $5,200 per year—for a grand total of $15,600. That's not very much, and by the time you are finished with the second job (not to mention the first), you are so exhausted, how can you tackle other things? Unfortunately, many single parents fall into the permanent minimum-wage trap. *Atlantic* magazine reports that a large number of single parents fall under the poverty line. Many end up trapped in the minimum-wage job situation and never get out of it! If you are in that type of trap, consider what options you might want to pursue for the long term. Seek help from those who want to better your lot.
5. Regardless of how you feel about his politics, there are some good lessons to learn from Pat Buchanan. When he graduated from college, he didn't merely choose the best offer that came along. He studied the future. He invested his time diligently researching different options. Then he chose what he thought would be the best outlet for his talents. He worked hard to get that particular job. When he got the job, he worked hard to excel from there. Since we spend *hours* and *hours* in the work force, why not spend some time in research at the front end, rather than settling for a momentous routine without hope for a better future?
6. Zig Ziglar, *See You at the Top,* 67.
7. Hebrews 9:27, KJV.

CHAPTER 10

1. Bliss, *Getting Things Done.*
2. Hebrews 12:3, NKJV.

3. Jim Elliot, quoted by D. James Kennedy, *A Matter of Profit and Loss* (Ft. Lauderdale, FL: Coral Ridge Ministries, 1984), 3.

4. I'm indebted to Earl Nightingale for this anecdote.

5. Lucy Hedrick, *Five Days to an Organized Life* (New York: Dell Publishing, 1990), 14.

6. Ibid., 17.

7. Proverbs 6:9–11.

CHAPTER 11

1. Will and Ariel Durant, *The Story of Civilization: Part X: Rousseau and Revolution* (New York: Simon and Schuster, 1967), 459–460.

2. 1 Corinthians 3:12–15.

3. Matthew 6:4, NKJV.

4. A paraphrase based on Matthew 25:14–30.

CHAPTER 12

1. Tan, *Encyclopedia of 7700 Illustrations,* (Rockville, MD: Assurance Publishers, 1984), 1089.

2. Charles Hummel, *Tyranny of the Urgent* (Downers Grove, IL: InterVarsity Press, 1967), 5.

3. Swenson, *Margin,* 14–15.

4. Ibid., 55.

5. Ibid., 83–87.

6. Ibid., 87.

EPILOGUE

1. 1 John 5:13 (paraphrase; emphasis mine).

2. Ecclesiastes 12:1.

3. 2 Corinthians 6:2, NKJV.

4. Isaiah 59:1–2.

5. Hebrews 10:31.

6. Hebrews 9:22.

7. Romans 3:23.

8. The address is Coral Ridge Ministries, Box 40, Ft. Lauderdale, FL 33302. Ask for *Beginning Again.*

INDEX

© Creators Syndicate, Inc.

also available from
JERRY NEWCOMBE

Inspired by renewed interest in classic stories of virtue, this collection of the world's greatest authors reminds us that exciting, entertaining, and inspiring stories can also support traditional Christian moral values. Each of the selections begins with a statement of the moral message and a suggestion on its suitability for young children. The range of subjects and writing styles makes this book a treasure of great literature for every audience.

0-8054-2009-6

available at fine bookstores everywhere